ACADEMIC VOCABULARY

Academic Words

Third Edition

Amy E. Olsen

Cuesta College

PEARSON
Longman

New York   San Francisco   Boston
London   Toronto   Sydney   Tokyo   Singapore   Madrid
Mexico City   Munich   Paris   Cape Town   Hong Kong   Montreal

To Katy and Dan

Thanks for fun times in the mountains, on the links, and around the kitchen table.

Acquisitions Editor: Melanie Craig
Associate Editor: Frederick Speers
Marketing Manager: Thomas DeMarco
Senior Supplements Editor: Donna Campion
Production Manager: Donna DeBenedictis
Project Coordination, Text Design, and Electronic Page Makeup: Elm Street Publishing Services, Inc.
Cover Designer/Manager: Wendy Ann Fredericks
Cover Photos: *Clockwise from top left:* Jeff Greenberg/The Image Works; Will and Deni McIntyre/Photo Researchers, Inc.; Charles Gupton/Stone/Getty Images; and Eric Meola/The Image Bank/Getty Images
Art Studios: Elm Street Publishing Services, Inc.; Gil Adams
Photo Researcher: Christine A. Pullo
Manufacturing Buyer: Lucy Hebard
Printer and Binder: Courier Corporation/Kendallville
Cover Printer: Coral Graphic Services

Photo Credits: p. 10 (L, R): The Everett Collection; **p. 16 (T):** Topham/The Image Works; **p. 16 (M):** Express/Getty Images; **p. 16 (B):** Chris Moorhouse; **p. 22:** Robert Brenner/PhotoEdit; **p. 24:** Amy E. Olsen; **p. 28 (T):** Hulton Archive/Getty Images; **p. 28 (B):** Mark Richards/PhotoEdit; **p. 36:** Antonio M. Rosano/Photographer's Choice/Getty Images; **p. 43:** Felicia Martinez/PhotoEdit, Inc.; **p. 46 (T):** Charles Gupton/Stone/Getty Images; **p. 46 (B):** Ilena Perlman/Stock, Boston; **p. 48:** David Young-Wolff/PhotoEdit; **p. 52:** Joe Sohm/ChromoSohm Media Inc./The Image Works; **p. 58 (T):** Robert Daly/Stone/Getty Images; **p. 58 (M):** Time/Life Pictures/Getty Images; **p. 58 (B):** Bettmann/Corbis; **p. 60:** Davis Barber/PhotoEdit; **p. 66:** Emma Lee/Life File/Getty Images; **p. 70 (T):** Al Campanie/Syracuse Newspapers/The Image Works; **p. 70 (M):** Chris Ladd/Taxi/Getty Images; **p. 70 (B):** Spike Mafford/Getty Images; **p. 76 (T):** John Elk/Stock, Boston; **p. 76 (B):** Carlos Navajas/The Image Bank/Getty Images; **p. 82 (T):** BP, NRSC/Photo Researchers, Inc.; **p. 82 (B):** Amy E. Olsen; **p. 84:** Paul A. Souders/CORBIS; **p. 86:** Amy E. Olsen; **p. 88:** David Young-Wolff/PhotoEdit; **p. 96:** John Lamb/Stone/Getty Images; **p. 100:** Comstock/SuperStock; **p. 104 (T):** Bill Aron/PhotoEdit; **p. 104 (B):** Digital Vision/Getty Images; **p. 112:** Jeff Greenberg/PhotoEdit; **p. 116 (T):** Vic Bider/PhotoEdit; **p. 116 (B):** Jeff Greenberg/PhotoEdit; **p. 118 (T):** David Weintraub/Photo Researchers; **p. 118 (M):** John Eastcott and Yva Momatiuk/The Image Works; **p. 118 (B):** John Serrao/Photo Researchers; **p. 126:** Michael Melford/National Geographic Society/Getty Images; **p. 130 (T):** Color Day Productions/Getty Images; **p. 130 (B):** Alan and Linda Detrick/Photo Researchers; **p. 136 (T):** Terry Vine/Stock/Getty Images; **p. 136 (B):** David Young-Wolff/PhotoEdit; **p. 138:** Getty Images; **p. 139:** Alan Carey/The Image Works; **p. 142 (T):** Spencer Arnold/Getty Images; **p. 142 (B):** AKG/Photo Researchers; **p. 148 (T):** Flying Colours Ltd./Digital Vision/Getty Images; **p. 148 (B):** Scott T. Baxter/Getty Images; **p. 157:** Corey Rich/Lonley Planet Images; **p. 160 (T):** Will and Deni McIntyre/Photo Researchers; **p. 160 (B):** Joe Drivas Photography; **p. 163:** Jeff Greenberg/PhotoEdit; **p. 166 (T):** David Hosking/Frank Lane Pictures/Photo Researchers; **p. 166 (B):** George H. H. Huey/CORBIS; **p. 169:** Topham/The Image Works; **p. 172:** Ricky John Malloy/Taxi/Getty Images; **p. 176 (T):** Burke/Triolo Productions/Brand X Pictures/Getty Images; **p. 176 (B):** Michael Newman/PhotoEdit; **p. 178 (T):** Eric Meola/The Image Bank/Getty Images; **p. 178 (B):** SPL/Photo Researchers; **p. 186:** Jeff Greenberg/The Image Works.

Please visit us at http://www.ablongman.com

ISBN 0-321-43952-X

3 4 5 6 7 8 9 10—CRK—09 08

CONTENTS

PREFACE

Because students benefit greatly from increased word power, the study of vocabulary should be enjoyable. Unfortunately, vocabulary workbooks often lose sight of this goal. To help make the study of vocabulary an exciting and enjoyable part of college study, I have written *Academic Vocabulary*.

The goal of this book—the third in a three-book interactive vocabulary series—is to make the study of vocabulary fun through a variety of thematic readings, self-tests, and interactive exercises. As a casual glimpse through the book will indicate, these activities involve writing, personal experience, art, and many other formats. The goal of these activities is simple: to utilize individual learning styles in order to help students learn new words in a large number of contexts.

Underlying the text's strong visual appeal is a strong underlying philosophy: an essential part of learning vocabulary is repeated exposure to a word. *Academic Vocabulary* provides eight exposures to each vocabulary word in the text plus more opportunities for exposure through the Collaborative Activities and games in the Instructor's Manual.

CONTENT OVERVIEW

Academic Vocabulary is an ideal text for both classroom and self-study. The twenty-four main chapters follow a specific and consistent format.

- **Thematic Reading:** Because most vocabulary is acquired through reading, each chapter, with the exception of the Word Parts and Review chapters, begins with a thematic reading that introduces ten vocabulary words in context. These readings come in a variety of formats, from newsletters to essays. The goal is to show that new words may be encountered anywhere. Rather than simply presenting a word list with definitions, students have the opportunity to discover the meanings of these new words via context clues.

  The themes for *Academic Vocabulary* were chosen from disciplines that most students will encounter at some point in their college careers. In choosing the words, I've been guided by four factors: (1) relation to the chapter theme; (2) use in textbooks, novels, magazines, and newspapers; (3) occurrence in standardized tests such as the SAT and GRE; and (4) my own experiences in teaching reading and writing.

- **Predicting:** The second page of each chapter contains a Predicting activity that gives students the chance to figure out the meaning of each vocabulary word before looking at its definition. The Predicting section helps students learn the value of context clues in determining a word's meaning. While the text does offer information on dictionary use, I strongly advocate the use of context clues as one of the most active methods of vocabulary development.

- **Self-Tests:** Following the Predicting activity are three Self-Tests in various formats. With these tests, students can monitor their comprehension. The tests include text and sentence completion, true/false situations, matching, and analogies. Some tests employ context clue strategies such as synonyms and antonyms and general meaning. Critical thinking skills are an important part of each test. (Answers to the Self-Tests appear in the Instructor's Manual.)

- **Word Wise:** Following the Self-Tests is the Word Wise section that teaches a variety of skills that are helpful to vocabulary acquisition. There are eight types of activities: Collaborative Activities, Internet Activities, Word Groups, Context Clue Mini-Lessons,

Where Did It Come From? (etymologies), Collocations, Word Pairs, and Connotations and Denotations. Each activity is explained in the Getting Started section. By doing these activities and reading more about how words are used, students will get additional practice and insight into the words they are learning.

- **Interactive Exercise:** Following the Word Wise section is an Interactive Exercise that asks the student to begin actively using the vocabulary words. The exercises may include writing, making lists, or answering questions. The Interactive Exercises give students the chance to really think about the meanings of the words, but, more importantly, they encourage students to begin using the words actively.

- **Hint:** Each chapter includes a hint for developing vocabulary, reading, or study skills. The hints are brief and practical, and students will be able to make use of them in all of their college courses.

- **Word List:** Following the Hint box is a list of the vocabulary words with a pronunciation guide, the part of speech, and a brief definition for each. I wrote these definitions with the idea of keeping them simple and nontechnical. Some vocabulary texts provide complicated dictionary definitions that include words students do not know; I've tried to make the definitions as friendly and as useful as possible.

- **Words to Watch:** This new section asks students to pick three–five words they may be having trouble with and write their own sentences using the words. This section is an additional chance for students to grasp the meaning of a few words that may be difficult for them.

ADDITIONAL FEATURES

In addition to the thematic vocabulary chapters, *Academic Vocabulary* includes a Getting Started chapter, three Word Parts chapters, three Review chapters, and a Flash Card section with instructions on how students can create their own flash cards.

- **Getting Started:** *Academic Vocabulary* begins with an introductory chapter to familiarize students with some of the tools of vocabulary acquisition. The "Parts of Speech" section gives sample words and sentences for the eight parts of speech. "Using the Dictionary" dissects a sample dictionary entry and provides an exercise for using guide words. "Completing Analogies" explains how analogies work, provides sample analogies, and gives students analogy exercises to complete. This section will prepare students for the analogy Self-Tests contained in several chapters of the text. The "Benefits of Flash Cards" section encourages students to make flash cards beginning with Chapter 1. The section explains the advantages of using flash cards and makes students aware of the "Create Your Own Flash Cards" section at the end of the text. The "Word Wise Features" section provides background information for the various Word Wise activities.

- **Word Parts:** The three Word Parts chapters introduce prefixes, roots, and suffixes used throughout the book. Students learn the meanings of these forms, and sample words illustrate the forms. Self-Tests in each Word Parts chapter give students the opportunity to practice using the word parts.

- **Review Chapters:** Three Review chapters focus on the preceding nine chapters. They divide the words into different activity groups and test students' cumulative knowledge. The words appear in artistic, test, written, puzzle, and collaborative formats. These repeated and varied exposures increase the likelihood that the students will remember the words, not just for one chapter or test, but for life.

- **Create Your Own Flash Cards:** The Create Your Own Flash Cards section teaches students how to make and use flash cards. Students can use the cards for self-study. Additionally, instructors can use them for the supplemental activities and games that are provided in the Instructor's Manual. Flash card templates are located in the back of the text. Students can photocopy the blank pages if they want to use this format, or they can use index cards as described in the flash card directions.

- **Word List:** The inside back cover features a list of all the vocabulary words and the page number on which the definition is given. A list of the word parts from the Word Parts chapters is also included on the inside back cover with page references.
- **Pronunciation Key:** On the inside front cover is a pronunciation key to help students understand the pronunciation symbols used in this text. The inside front cover also offers some additional guidelines on pronunciation issues.

FEATURES NEW TO THIS EDITION

This edition of the text has several new features in response to instructor comments. The new materials and organization of the book have been employed to make the text more appealing to students and easier for instructors to use.

- **Refined In-Chapter Organization:** The Word List is now at the end of each chapter, so students can do the Predicting exercise without accidentally looking at the Word List below. The last page of each chapter contains the Word List and the Words to Watch exercise. Instructors can now have students rip out the Self-Tests to hand in and not lose the thematic reading for the next chapter.
- **Added Content:** The new Words to Watch exercises give students extra practice with words they are having difficulty with. The Word Wise sections introduce important vocabulary concepts and activities to increase student interest in learning new words. A list of the Word Parts introduced in the text has been added to the Word List on the inside back cover, so instructors and students can easily find a word part they want to review.
- **New Readings:** Some chapters have been updated to deal with themes more relevant to students. Several chapters have also been lengthened to give students more reading practice and to increase a student's cultural literacy about a topic. Additionally, new words have been added to several chapters.
- **Updated Analogies Section:** The Analogies Appendix has been moved to the Getting Started chapter to allow students a chance to work with analogies before they start the Self-Tests. The section has been renamed "Completing Analogies," and it offers greater explanation on how to complete analogies and offers practice exercises.
- **Hints:** A Hint box has been added to every chapter. The hints deal with improving vocabulary, reading, and study skills. The hints are brief and practical, and students will be able to make use of them in many of their college courses.
- **Updated CD-ROM:** The CD-ROM that accompanies *Academic Vocabulary* has been updated to include more effective and relevant exercises.

THE TEACHING AND LEARNING PACKAGE

Each component of the teaching and learning package for *Academic Vocabulary* has been carefully crafted to maximize the main text's value.

- **Instructor's Manual and Test Bank:** The Instructor's Manual and Test Bank, which is almost as long as the main text, includes options for additional Collaborative Activities and games. The collaborative section explains ways students can share their work on the Interactive Exercises in pairs, in small groups, or with the whole class. Ideas for other collaborative activities using different learning styles are also offered. The games section presents games that can be used with individual chapters or for review of several chapters. Some of the games are individual; others are full-class activities. Some games have winners, and some are just for fun. The games may involve acting, drawing, or writing. The Collaborative Activities and games give students the opportunity to use the words in conversational settings and a chance to work with others.

The Test Bank, formatted for easy copying, includes two tests for each chapter as well as combined tests of two to three chapters. There are also Mastery Tests to accompany the Review chapters and full-book Mastery Tests that can be used as final exams. ISBN: 0-321-44622-4.

- *Academic Vocabulary* **Study Wizard CD-ROM:** In the computer age many students enjoy learning via computers. Available with this text is the *Academic Vocabulary* Study Wizard CD-ROM, which features additional exercises and tests that provide for even more interaction between the students and the words. The CD-ROM has an audio component that allows students to hear each chapter's thematic reading and the pronunciation of each word as often as they choose. Students are often reluctant to use the new words they learn because they aren't sure how to pronounce them. The pronunciation guides in each chapter do help to address this fear, but actually hearing the words spoken will give students greater confidence in using the words. Contact your Longman publishing representative to order the student text packaged with the CD-ROM for an additional $3.00.

FOR ADDITIONAL READING AND REFERENCE

The Longman Basic Skills Package

In addition to the book-specific supplements discussed above, many other skills-based supplements are available for both instructors and students. All of these supplements are available either at no additional cost or at greatly reduced prices.

- **The Dictionary Deal.** Two dictionaries can be shrink-wrapped with *Academic Vocabulary* at a nominal fee. *The New American Webster Handy College Dictionary* is a paperback reference text with more than 100,000 entries. *Merriam-Webster's Collegiate Dictionary,* Eleventh Edition, is a hardback reference with a citation file of more than 14.5 million examples of English words drawn from actual use. For more information on how to shrink-wrap a dictionary with your text, please contact your Longman publishing representative.
- **Longman Vocabulary Web Site.** For additional vocabulary-related resources, visit our free vocabulary Web site at http://www.ablongman.com/vocabulary.
- **MyReadingLab (www.myreadinglab.com).** MyReadingLab, where better reading skills are within reach, is a collection of reading, vocabulary, and study skills activities consolidated into a central suite. At the heart of MyReadingLab is the interactive tutorial system Reading Road Trip, the most widely used reading tutorial software. Reading Road Trip takes students on a tour of 16 landmarks in different cities throughout the United States; at each attraction students learn and practice a different reading skill while absorbing the local color. MyReadingLab also includes access to the Longman Vocabulary Web site, Longman Study Skills Web site, and Research Navigator.

ACKNOWLEDGMENTS

I want to thank the following reviewers for their helpful suggestions as the book took shape for both the first and second editions: Kathy Beggs, Pikes Peak Community College; Diane Bosco, Suffolk County Community College; Janet Curtis, Fullerton College; Carol E. Dietrick, Miami-Dade Community College; Patrice Haydell, Delgado Community College; Miriam A. Kinard, Trident Technical College; Belinda Klau, Imperial Valley College; John M. Kopec, Boston University; Maggi Miller, Austin Community College; Susan Sandmeier, Columbia Basin College; Kerry Segel, Saginaw

Valley State University; Kathleen Sneddon, University of Nebraska, Lincoln; Shirley Wachtel, Middlesex County College; and Carolyn J. Wilkie, Indiana University of Pennsylvania.

And for the third edition, my thanks go to Kathy Beggs, Pikes Peak Community College; Janie Emerson, Miami Dade College; Joycelyn Jacobs, Lee College; Anne Lewald, Tennessee Tech University; Dan Purtscher, Pikes Peak Community College; and Laurel S. Watt, Inver Hills Community College.

Additionally, I want to thank Frederick Speers, Associate Editor of Basic Skills at Longman, for his help in organizing this edition. Commendations go to the Supplement and Marketing departments of Longman for their efforts on different aspects of the book. Many thanks also go to those at Elm Street Publishing Services for making this series visually appealing. I am grateful to several colleagues across California for our significant discussions on reading and writing at diverse conferences and other gatherings. Finally, I offer my deepest appreciation to family and friends who have been encouraging over the years.

I am proud to present the third edition of *Academic Vocabulary,* a book that continues to make learning vocabulary fun and meaningful.

—AMY E. OLSEN

ALSO AVAILABLE

Book 1 of the Vocabulary Series:
   Interactive Vocabulary: General Words by Amy E. Olsen

Book 2 of the Vocabulary Series:
   Active Vocabulary: General and Academic Words by Amy E. Olsen

TO THE STUDENT

This book is designed to make learning vocabulary fun. You will increase the benefits of this book if you keep a few points in mind.

1. **Interact with the words.** Each chapter contains eight exposures to a word, and your instructor may introduce one or two additional activities. If you're careful in your reading and thorough in doing the activities for each chapter, learning the words will be fun and easy.

2. **Appreciate the importance of words.** The words for the readings were picked from textbooks in a variety of academic disciplines, magazines, newspapers, novels, and lists of words likely to appear on standardized tests (such as the SAT and GRE). These are words you will encounter in the classroom and in everyday life. Learning these words will help you be a more informed citizen and will make your academic life much richer. Even if you don't currently have an interest in one of the readings, keep an open mind: the words may appear in the article you read in tomorrow's newspaper or on an exam in one of next semester's classes. The readings also come in different formats as a reminder that you can learn new vocabulary anywhere, from a newsletter to a memo.

3. **Find your preferred learning style.** This book aims to provide exercises for all types of learners—visual, aural, and interpersonal. But only you can say which learning style works best for you. See which activities (drawings, acting, matching, completing stories) you like most, and replicate those activities when they aren't part of a chapter.

4. **Value critical thinking.** The variety of exercise formats you will find in the following pages make the book fun to work with and build a range of critical thinking skills. For example, the analogies will help you see relationships between words, the fill-in-the-blank formats will aid you in learning to put words in context, and the True/False Self-Tests will focus your attention on whether words are used correctly in a sentence. Each type of activity will be developing your critical thinking skills while building your vocabulary.

5. **Remember that learning is fun.** Don't make a chore out of learning new words, or any other new skill for that matter. If you enjoy what you're doing, you're more likely to welcome the information and to retain it.

Enjoy your journey through *Academic Vocabulary!*

—AMY E. OLSEN

ACADEMIC VOCABULARY

Getting Started

▌▐▐▌▌ PARTS OF SPEECH

There are eight parts of speech. A word's part of speech is based on how the word is used in a sentence. Words can, therefore, be more than one part of speech. For an example, note how the word *punch* is used below.

nouns: (n.) name a person, place, or thing

    EXAMPLES: Ms. Lopez, New Orleans, lamp, warmth

    Ms. Lopez enjoyed her *trip* to *New Orleans* where she bought a beautiful *lamp*. The *warmth* of the *sun* filled *Claire* with *happiness*. I drank five *cups* of the orange *punch*.

pronouns: (pron.) take the place of a noun

    EXAMPLES: I, me, you, she, he, it, her, we, they, my, which, that, anybody, everybody

    Everybody liked the music at the party. *It* was the kind that made people want to dance. *They* bought a new car, *which* hurt their bank account.

verbs: (v.) express an action or state of being

    EXAMPLES: enjoy, run, think, read, dance, am, is, are, was, were

    Lily *read* an interesting book yesterday. I *am* tired. He *is* an excellent student. She *punched* the bully.

adjectives: (adj.) modify (describe or explain) a noun or pronoun

    EXAMPLES: pretty, old, two, expensive, red, small

    The *old* car was covered with *red* paint on *one* side. The *two* women met for lunch at an *expensive* restaurant. The *punch* bowl was empty soon after Uncle Al got to the party.

adverbs: (adv.) modify a verb, an adjective, or another adverb

    EXAMPLES: very, shortly, first, too, soon, quickly, finally, furthermore, however

    We will meet *shortly* after one o'clock. The *very* pretty dress sold *quickly*. I liked her; *however,* there was something strange about her.

prepositions: (prep.) are placed before a noun or pronoun to create a phrase that relates to other parts of the sentence

    EXAMPLES: after, around, at, before, by, from, in, into, of, off, on, through, to, up, with

    He told me to be *at* his house *in* the afternoon. You must go *through* all the steps to do the job.

conjunctions: (conj.) join words or other sentence elements and show a relationship between the connected items

    EXAMPLES: and, but, or, nor, for, so, yet, after, although, because, if, since, than, when

    I went to the movies, *and* I went to dinner on Tuesday. I will not go to the party this weekend *because* I have to study. I don't want to hear your reasons *or* excuses.

interjections: (interj.) show surprise or emotion

    EXAMPLES: oh, hey, wow, ah, ouch

    Oh, I forgot to do my homework! *Wow,* I got an A on the test!

USING THE DICTIONARY

There will be times when you need to use a dictionary for one of its many features; becoming familiar with dictionary **entries** will make using a dictionary more enjoyable. The words in a dictionary are arranged alphabetically. The words on a given page are signaled by **guide words** at the top of the page. If the word you are looking for comes alphabetically between these two words then your word is on that page.

1436

wing tip • wintry ← Guide words

Entry

wing tip *n* (ca. 1908) **1a** : the edge or outer margin of a bird's wing **b** *usu* **wingtip** : the outer end of an airplane wing **2** : a toe cap having a point that extends back toward the throat of the shoe and curving sides that extend toward the shank **3** : a shoe having a wing tip

¹**wink**\'wiŋk\ *vb* [ME, fr. OE *wincian;* akin to OHG *winchan* to stagger, wink and perh. to L *vacillare* to sway, Skt *vañcati* he goes crookedly] *vi* (bef. 12c) **1** : to shut one eye briefly as a signal or in teasing **2** : to close and open the eyelids quickly **3** : to avoid seeing or noting something — usu. used with *at* **4** : to gleam or flash intermittently: TWINKLE <her glasses *~ing* in the sunlight — Harper Lee> **5 a** : to come to an end — usu. used with *out* **b** : to stop shining — usu. used with *out* **6** : to signal a message with a light ~ *vt* **1** : to cause to open and shut **2** : to affect or influence by or as if by blinking the eyes

²**wink** *n* (14c) **1** : a brief period of sleep : NAP <catching a ~> **2 a** : a hint or sign given by winking **b** : an act of winking **3** : the time of a wink: INSTANT <quick as a ~> **4** : a flicker of the eyelids: BLINK

wink·er \'wiŋ-kər\ *n* (1549) **1** : one that winks **2** : a horse's blinder

¹**win·kle** \'wiŋ-kəl\ *n* [by shortening] (1585) : ²PERIWINKLE

²**winkle** *vi* **win·kled; win·kling** \-k(ə-)liŋ\ [freq. of *wink*] (1791): TWINKLE

³**winkle** *vt* **win·kled; win·kling** \-k(ə-)liŋ\ [¹*winkle;* fr. the process of extracting a winkle from its shell] (1918) **1** *chiefly Brit* : to displace, remove, or evict from a position — usu. used with *out* **2** *chiefly Brit* : to obtain or draw out by effort — usu. used with *out* <no attempt to ~ out why they do it — Joan Bakewell>

win·ner\ 'wi-nər\ *n* (14c) : one that wins: as **a** : one that is successful esp. through praiseworthy ability and hard work **b** : a victor esp. in games and sports **c** : one that wins admiration **d** : a shot in a court game that is not returned and that scores for the player making it

win·ter·ize \'win-tə-,rīz\ *vt* **-ized ; -iz·ing** (1934) : to make ready for winter or winter use and esp. resistant or proof against winter weather <~ a car> — **win·ter·i·za·tion** \,win-tə-rə-'zā-shən\ *n*

win·ter—kill \'win-tər-,kil\ *vt* (ca. 1806) : to kill (as a plant) by exposure to winter conditions ~ *vi* : to die as a result of exposure to winter conditions — **winterkill** *n*

win·ter·ly \'win-tər-lē\ *adj* (1559) : of, relating to, or occurring in winter : WINTRY

winter melon *n* (ca. 1900) **1** : any of several muskmelons (as a casaba or honeydew melon) that are fruits of a cultivated vine (*Cucumis melo indorus*) **2** : a large white-fleshed melon that is the fruit of an Asian vine (*Benincasa hispida*) and is used esp. in Chinese cooking

winter quarters *n pl but sing or pl in constr* (1641) : a winter residence or station (as of a military unit or a circus)

winter savory *n* (1597) : a perennial European mint (*Satureja montana*) with leaves used for seasoning — compare SUMMER SAVORY

winter squash *n* (1775) : any of various hard-shelled squashes that belong to cultivars derived from several species (esp. *Cucurbita maxima, C. moschata,* and *C. pepo*) and that can be stored for several months

win·ter·tide \'win-tər-,tīd\ *n* (bef. 12c) : WINTERTIME

win·ter·time \-,tīm\ *n* (14c) : the season of winter

win through *vi* (1644) : to survive difficulties and reach a desired or satisfactory end <*win through* to a better life beyond — B. F. Reilly>

win·tle \'wi-nᵊl,'win-tᵊl\ *vi* **win·tled; win·tling** \'win(t)-liŋ; 'wi-nᵊl-iŋ, 'win-tᵊl-\ [perh. fr. D dial. *windtelen* to reel] (1786) **1** *Scot* : STAGGER, REEL **2** *Scot* : WRIGGLE

win·try \'win-trē\ *also* **win·tery** \'win-t(ə-)rē\ *adj* **win·tri·er; -est** (bef. 12c) **1** : of, relating to, or characteristic of winter **2 a** : weathered by or as if by winter : AGED, HOARY **b** : CHEERLESS, CHILLING <a ~ greeting> — **win·tri·ness** \'win-trē-nəs\ *n*

SOURCE: By permission. From *Merriam-Webster's Collegiate® Dictionary, Eleventh Edition* © 2004 by Merriam-Webster, Incorporated (www.Merriam-Webster.com).

© 2007 Pearson Education, Inc.

Most dictionaries contain the following information in an entry:

- The **pronunciation**—symbols show how a word should be spoken, including how the word is divided into syllables and where the stress should be placed on a word. The Pronunciation Key for this book is located on the inside front cover. The key shows the symbols used to indicate the sound of a word. Every dictionary has a pronunciation method and a pronunciation key or guide is usually found in the front pages, with a partial key at the bottom of each page. The differences in the pronunciation systems used by dictionaries are usually slight.
- The **part of speech**—usually abbreviated, such as *n.* for noun, *v.* for verb, and *adj.* for adjective. A key to these abbreviations and others is usually found in the front of the dictionary.
- The **definition**—usually the most common meaning is listed first followed by other meanings.
- An **example of the word in a sentence**—the sentence is usually in italics and follows each meaning.
- **Synonyms** and **antonyms**—*synonyms* are words with similar meanings, and *antonyms* are words with opposite meanings. (You should also consider owning a **thesaurus,** a book that lists synonyms and antonyms.)
- The **etymology**—the history of a word, usually including the language(s) it came from.
- The **spelling of different forms** of the word—these forms may include unusual plurals and verb tenses (especially irregular forms).

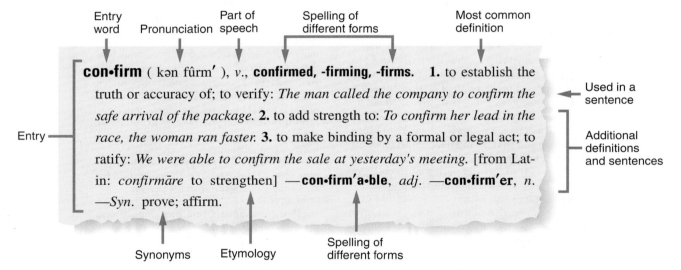

When choosing a dictionary, take the time to look at different dictionaries and see what appeals to you. Dictionaries come in several sizes and are made for different purposes. First read some of the entries and see if the definitions make sense to you. See which of the features above are used in the dictionary. Is it important to you to be able to study the etymology of a word? Would you like sample sentences? Some dictionaries have illustrations in the margins. Decide if that is a feature you would use. Check to see if the print is large enough for you to read easily.

Decide on how you will use this dictionary. Do you want a paperback dictionary to put in your backpack? Or is this going to be the dictionary for your desk and a large hardback version would be the better choice? Several disciplines have specialized dictionaries with meanings that apply to those fields, such as law or medicine. There are also bilingual dictionaries, such as French/English or Spanish/English that can be helpful for school or travel. Take time in picking out your dictionary because a good dictionary will be a companion for years to come. A few dictionaries to consider are *Merriam-Webster's Collegiate Dictionary, The American Heritage Dictionary, The Random House College Dictionary,* and *The Oxford Dictionary.*

In general, when you are reading try to use context clues, the words around the word you don't know, to first figure out the meaning of a word, but if you are still in doubt don't hesitate to refer to a dictionary for the exact definition. Don't forget that dictionaries also contain more than definitions and are an essential reference source for any student.

▚▚▚ USING GUIDE WORDS

Use the sample guide words to determine on which page each of the ten words will be found. Write the page number next to the entry word.

Page	Guide Words
157	bone/boo
159	boot/born
435	endemic/endorse
654	humanist/humongous
655	humor/hunter
975	pamphlet/pandemonium
976	pander/pant
1480	velvet/venom

Example: _654_ humdinger

_____ 1. pang

_____ 2. Panama

_____ 3. bonnet

_____ 4. vengeance

_____ 5. endive

_____ 6. hunk

_____ 7. booth

_____ 8. pansy

_____ 9. humanoid

_____ 10. hummus

▚▚▚ ENTRY IDENTIFICATION

Label the parts of the following entry.

① ② ③ ④ ⑤

a•ble (ā′ bəl) *adj.* **a•bler, a•blest.** 1. having the necessary power, skill, or qualifications to do something: *She was able to read music.* **⑥**

⑦ 2. having or showing unusual talent, intelligence, skill, or knowledge: *Washington was an able leader.* [1275–1325; ME < MF < L **⑧** *habilis* easy to handle, adaptable=*hab(ēre)* to have, hold + *ilis* –ile] Syn. apt, talented.

⑨

1. _____

2. _____

3. _____

4. _____

5. _____

6. _____

7. _____

8. _____

9. _____

▌▐█▌ COMPLETING ANALOGIES

An **analogy** shows a relationship between words. Working with analogies helps one to see connections between items, which is a crucial critical thinking skill. Analogies are written as follows: big : large :: fast : quick. The colon (:) means *is to*. The analogy reads big *is to* large as fast *is to* quick. To complete analogies

1. find a relationship between the first pair of words

2. look for a similar relationship in another set of words

In the example above *big* and *large* have similar meanings; they are synonyms. *Fast* and *quick* also have similar meanings, so the relationship between the four words uses synonyms.

Common relationships used in analogies (with examples) include

synonyms (trip : journey)	grammatical structure (shaking : shivering)
antonyms (real : fake)	cause and effect (step in a puddle : get wet)
examples (strawberry : fruit)	sequences (turn on car : drive)
part to a whole (handle : cup)	an object to a user or its use (spatula : chef)

Analogies in this book come in matching and fill-in-the-blank forms. Try the following analogies for practice.

▌▐██ MATCHING

1. old : young :: _____   a. preface : book

2. clip coupons : go shopping :: _____   b. put on shoes : take a walk

3. peel : banana :: _____   c. low wages : strike

4. no rain : drought :: _____   d. rested : tired

▌▐██ FILL-IN-THE-BLANK

writer	passion	abduct	sadly

5. frozen : chilled :: kidnap : _____

6. interrupting : rude :: embracing : _____

7. slow : slowly :: sad : _____

8. baton : conductor :: computer : _____

ANSWERS

1. To figure out this analogy first one needs to see that *old* and *young* are opposites or **antonyms.** Next look at the choices and see if another pair of words are antonyms, and, yes, *rested* and *tired* are opposites. The answer is d.
2. A person would *clip coupons* and then *go shopping,* so there is a **sequence** of events. Of the choices, one would *put on shoes* and then *take a walk,* another sequence. The answer is b.
3. A *peel* is a part of a *banana,* while a *preface* is part of a *book,* so the connection is **part to a whole.** The answer is a.
4. When an area gets *no rain* it can lead to a *drought,* and when people get paid *low wages,* they can go on *strike.* The connection among these pairs is **cause and effect.** The answer is c.
5. *Frozen* and *chilled* have similar meanings; they are **synonyms.** To solve the analogy, pick a word that has a similar meaning to *kidnap,* which would be *abduct.*
6. *Interrupting* a person is **an example** of a *rude* behavior. *Embracing* is an example of another type of behavior; in this case, it fits as an example of *passion.*
7. *Slow* is an adjective and *slowly* an adverb; *sad* is an adjective and *sadly* an adverb. This analogy works by using the same **grammatical structure** between the words.
8. A *baton* is used by a *conductor.* Who uses a *computer?* Among the choices, *writer* obviously fits. The relationship here is **object to user.**

Sometimes you may come up with a relationship between the first two words that makes sense, but doesn't fit any of the choices. Look at the choices and the two words again to see if you can find a way any four words fit together. Also do any obvious matches first, and with fewer choices it will be easier to spot the harder connections. Doing analogies can be fun as you begin to make clever connections and see word relationships in new ways. Finding word connections will help your brain make other connections in areas as diverse as writing essays, doing math problems, and arranging travel plans. Analogies are just another way to exercise your thinking skills.

Try a few more analogies and check your answers on page 12 to see how you did.

MATCHING

1. button : shirt ::	_____	a. broom : janitor
2. map : traveler ::	_____	b. drawer : desk
3. calm : tranquil ::	_____	c. stayed up late : exhausted
4. watched a comedy : laughed ::	_____	d. wise : smart

FILL-IN-THE-BLANK

huge	beverage	warmth	sleep

5. make dinner : eat :: put on pajamas : ____________________
6. dull : bright :: tiny : ____________________
7. trunk : storage :: coat : ____________________
8. the Nile : a river :: iced tea : ____________________

■|■■■ BENEFITS OF FLASH CARDS

There are several benefits to using flash cards to help you study vocabulary words.

Making the Cards The first benefit comes from just making the cards. When you make a card, you will practice writing the word and its definition. You may also write a sentence using the word, record its part of speech, or draw a picture of the word. See the section "Create Your Own Flash Cards" on page 190 at the back of this book for ideas on how to make flash cards. Creating the cards allows for a personal experience with the words, which makes learning the words easier.

Working with Others Another benefit is that using the cards can lead to collaborative activities. When you ask a friend, family member, or classmate to quiz you on the words, you get the chance to work with someone else, which many people enjoy. You may even establish a study group with the friends you find from quizzing each other on your flash cards.

Evaluating Your Learning A third benefit is that the cards serve as pre-tests that let you evaluate how well you know a word. When a friend quizzes you, ask him or her to go over the words you miss several times. As the stack of flash cards with words you don't know gets smaller, you know that the words are becoming part of your vocabulary. You know that you are prepared to face a word on a quiz or test when you can correctly give the definition several times.

Making and using the flash cards should be fun. Enjoy the process of learning new words. Turn to the back of the book now to review the directions for creating flash cards, and you will be ready to make cards beginning with Chapter 1. You can use the templates provided at the end of the book to get started.

■|■■■ WORD WISE FEATURES

The Word Wise boxes share information on different areas related to vocabulary. There are eight types of features.

Collaborative Activity presents different ways to interact with the vocabulary words, especially using a variety of learning styles such as music and movement.

Internet Activity suggests ways to use technology to enhance your learning experience.

Word Groups explains how putting words into related groups can help your mind organize new vocabulary.

Context Clue Mini-Lessons provide different types of context clue situations and give you the opportunity to practice using each type. *Context* means the words surrounding a specific word that give clues to that word's meaning. When you encounter a word whose meaning you don't know, keep reading the passage, looking for clues to help you figure out the meaning. These clues might be in the same sentence as the unknown words or in a sentence that comes before or after the word. Look for these types of clues in a passage:

Synonyms—words that have a similar meaning to the unknown word

Antonyms—words that mean the opposite of the unknown word

Examples—a list of items that explain the unknown word

General meaning—the meaning of the sentence or passage as a whole that could clarify the meaning of the unknown word

Each type of context clue has a mini-lesson and a final lesson combines the methods. You will not find a context clue every time you encounter a word you don't know, but being aware of context clues will help you determine the meaning of many new words and make reading more enjoyable.

Where Did It Come From?   presents interesting etymologies (word histories). Some of the histories use the word parts presented in the three Word Parts chapters of the text.

Collocations   show ways words are used together. The groupings can come in several forms, such as a verb with a noun (*commit* a *crime*), and adjective with a noun (*handsome stranger*), or a verb with a preposition (*come over*). Learning collocations will help you understand common ways to use the words you are studying. Sentences with the collocations in italics for some of the vocabulary words in this text are spread throughout the chapters. To become more familiar with collocations, look and listen for other repeated word combinations in the materials you read, in the phrases people use when speaking, and as you do the self-tests in this book.

Word Pairs   illustrate how some words are often used near each other. Learning word pairs can help you to better remember both words. Some words are pairs because the items they represent are often used together, such as peanut butter and jelly. Other word pairs are opposites that are often found together when describing objects, actions, or people (such as "My friends are as different as night and day"). Word pairs are presented in several chapters with sample sentences to show how the words can be used near each other.

Connotations and Denotations   examine reactions to a word. A **denotation** is "the explicit or direct meaning of a word." This is the kind of definition you would find in the dictionary. A **connotation** is "the suggestive or associative meaning of a word beyond its literal definition." This is the emotional response you have to a word. (A mnemonic device for remembering the difference between the two is that denotation begins with a "d," and it is the dictionary or direct meaning, both beginning with a "d").

It is important to realize that words have two kinds of meanings because careful writers use both kinds. You, as a writer and reader, want to make sure you are clearly expressing your point and understanding another writer's ideas by recognizing how words are used. Some connotations are personal reactions. For example, *seclusion* means "solitude; a sheltered place." Depending on your personality or current living conditions, you might picture *seclusion* as a wonderful chance to be alone and relax without all the chaos surrounding you, or if you hate being by yourself, you may envision it as a kind of torture separating you from friends and family. Other connotations have broader emotional responses. If you wanted to describe a thin person you could use the words *slender* or *scrawny*. What do you picture in your mind for each word? Talk to your classmates about their images. Are they similar? Some words have positive connotations that people feel good about and other words have negative connotations that turn people off. Not all words have strong connotations. For most people a pencil is a pencil, and there isn't much to get excited about. But other words can bring out strong feelings, such as *frugal*. The Connotation and Denotation lessons look at some of the vocabulary words in this text and the differences in their meanings.

Well Worth Watching

Classic Movie Corner

If you are looking for a great movie to spend time with this weekend, here are two classics that won't disappoint you, even if you have seen them before.

Psycho (1960)

5   *Wild Strawberries* (1957)

Ingmar Bergman's *Wild Strawberries* has been **hailed** as a
10   masterpiece, and it is a film that deserves its reputation. Bergman wrote
15   and directed the film. The movie takes viewers into the mind of Isak Borg, an elderly gentleman, as he embarks on a long car trip to receive an honorary degree. The **cinematography** brilliantly uses black-and-white contrasts to show his
20   disturbed thoughts. **Surreal** dream sequences take us into his past and into his **disconcerted** mind. Clocks without hands and an examination room with strange questions are among the unusual experiences Dr. Borg faces. The
25   **juxtapositions** of old age and youth (both Borg's youth and the young people he meets on his journey) force us, as well as the doctor, to examine life and our actions. As this is a film you will want to discuss after viewing, invite your
30   friends over to share ideas on what the dream sequences might mean and what Bergman may have wanted people to gain from seeing the movie.

The film stars Victor Sjostrom, Bibi Andersson,
35   Ingrid Thulin, Gunnar Bjornstand, and Max Von Sydow. Swedish. 90 minutes.

Alfred Hitchcock's films are a must for the **connoisseur** of the suspense **genre**, and *Psycho* is one of his best films. Whether you have seen it
40   once, twice, or a hundred times it is worth another viewing, and if you have never seen it, it is about time you did. Hitchcock was marvelously **attuned** to the darker sides of human nature, and he was
45   able to convey the fears and desires of lust and greed in fascinating images. In the famous shower scene, for example, Hitchcock uses **montage** to create the suspense. Through careful editing, he creates tension in the audience while barely
50   showing the plunging knife touch the victim. In fact, Hitchcock put seventy-eight short shots together to create the scene. For many people, *Psycho* **epitomizes** the suspense movie. It holds all the thrills an audience expects from the
55   unexpected. Hitchcock masterfully used lighting, camera movements, and music to create the terror one craves in a suspense movie, unlike many of the disappointing horror films of today that reveal too much, too fast, and too predictably. Norman Bates continues to reign as one of the scariest
60   characters in film history.

The film stars Anthony Perkins, Vera Miles, John Gavin, Martin Balsam, John McIntire, and Janet Leigh. American. 108 minutes.

PREDICTING

For each set, write the definition on the line next to the word to which it belongs. If you are unsure, return to the reading on page 10, and underline any context clues you find. After you've made your predictions, check your answers against the Word List on page 15. Place a checkmark in the box next to each word whose definition you missed. These are the words you'll want to study closely.

SET ONE

fantastic	approved enthusiastically	disturbed
the art of motion picture photography	the act of placing close together	

☐ 1. **hailed** (line 9) _____

☐ 2. **cinematography** (line 18) _____

☐ 3. **surreal** (line 20) _____

☐ 4. **disconcerted** (line 21) _____

☐ 5. **juxtapositions** (line 25) _____

SET TWO

a style	a film editing technique	a person who can judge the best in a field
serves as a typical or perfect example of	adjusted	

☐ 6. **connoisseur** (line 39) _____

☐ 7. **genre** (line 39) _____

☐ 8. **attuned** (line 43) _____

☐ 9. **montage** (line 47) _____

☐ 10. **epitomizes** (line 53) _____

SELF-TESTS

1 Circle the correct meaning of each vocabulary word.

1. hail:	welcome	ignore
2. connoisseur:	unsure of quality	judge of the best
3. genre:	a style	an exception
4. montage:	separate	combining to form a whole
5. attune:	adjust	clash
6. epitomize:	typify	conceal
7. disconcerted:	clear	confused
8. surreal:	fantastic	factual

9. cinematography: art of writing   art of motion picture photography

10. juxtaposition: putting far apart   placing close together

2 These comments are overheard as people file out of the multiplex movie theater. Match each sentence to the word it best fits. Use each word once.

VOCABULARY LIST

genre	surreal	attuned	disconcerted	juxtaposition
montage	hail	epitomize	connoisseur	cinematography

1. "The desert scenes were beautifully filmed. They really showed the richness of color in the sand and the sunsets." _____

2. "That was a great film! It's going to be the year's best movie!" _____

3. "Even though it was so strange, I liked it when everyone started flying around and speaking that strange language." _____

4. "I had to get used to the relaxed pace of the movie, but once I did, I really enjoyed the film." _____

5. "I am an expert on horror movies, and I can tell you this was not one of the director's best efforts." _____

6. "It really disturbed me when the movie began jumping back and forth between the past and the present." _____

7. "Next time we are staying home and renting Westerns; those are my kinds of movies." _____

8. "It was interesting how the blonde woman was standing next to old cars in so many scenes. I think the director was trying to make a point about stereotypes in America." _____

9. "That film is a perfect example of everything I dislike about musicals, especially having people break into a song every ten minutes." _____

10. "I liked the part where the director put the various shots of prison life together to show the boredom of the prisoners." _____

Answers to the analogies practice in the Getting Started section on page 7:
1. b 2. a 3. d 4. c 5. sleep 6. huge 7. warmth 8. beverage

3 Finish the sentences. Use each word once.

VOCABULARY LIST

epitomized	attuned	connoisseur	surreal	juxtaposition
montage	hailed	disconcerted	genre	cinematography

1. My father is a chocolate _____; he will eat nothing but the finest European chocolates.

2. My favorite movie _____ is the musical, but my husband prefers horror movies.

3. The _____ of scenes on a quiet beach with the freeway traffic really showed that the character needed to escape the pressures of the big city.

4. The vivid colors used in the film caused me to pay attention to the _____ over the other elements such as music and plot.

5. By being _____ to the latest trends, some producers can create a movie that capitalizes on a fad such as skateboarding or disco dancing.

6. It is easy to become _____ in today's multiplex theaters; I went to get popcorn and couldn't find my way back without asking an usher for directions.

7. The newspaper reviewer loved the concert; she _____ it as the best performance in the symphony's twenty-year history.

8. In *Battleship Potemkin*, Eisenstein's skillful editing of scenes showing the poor treatment of the sailors creates a powerful _____ that depicts the men's discontent.

9. The scene where the man threw the puppy off the roof _____ his evil nature.

10. It was a(n) _____ experience when I woke up in a hotel room and thought I was in my own bedroom.

WORD WISE

Context Clue Mini-Lesson 1

This lesson features synonyms—words that have a similar meaning to the unknown word. In the paragraph below, circle the synonyms you find for the underlined words and write them on the lines that follow the paragraph.

The <u>din</u> in the convention hall was deafening. Every vendor loudly <u>touted</u> the benefits of his or her product. The sellers pushed their products with phrases like the "best knife ever" or "lose ten pounds overnight." My friend admired the <u>pluck</u> of the sellers, but their shouts were nothing but noise to me. Many people also seemed to appreciate the spirited calls of the vendors as they gathered round to watch a demonstration. On the other hand, I began to <u>rue</u> the day I let my friend talk me into coming. My regret increased when in a weak moment I bought a hammer that was supposed to pound a nail with one blow.

The Synonym

1. Din _____

2. Touted _____

3. Pluck _____

4. Rue _____

Answer the following questions.

1. What is your favorite movie genre? _____

2. What might happen in a surreal dream?_____

_____

3. What would look unusual juxtaposed next to a piece of fruit?_____

_____

4. What are you a connoisseur of or what would you like to be a connoisseur of?

_____

5. What can you do to be better attuned to the feelings of others?_____

_____

_____

6. Which movie star do you think epitomizes style? _____

7. What movie do you think has beautiful cinematography?_____

_____

8. What could happen in a movie to make you feel disconcerted?_____

_____

_____

9. What would you hail as a great achievement of humankind?_____

_____

_____

10. If you were to create a montage showing the first day of kindergarten, what are three images you would use?_____

_____

_____

HINT

Flash Cards

Flash cards are a great way to study vocabulary. Turn to the "Create Your Own Flash Cards" section at the end of this book (page 190) for suggestions on ways to make and use flash cards. Remember to carry your flash cards with you and study for at least a few minutes each day. Also ask classmates, friends, and family members to quiz you using the flash cards. There are a few templates to get you started at the end of this book. Make copies of them before you fill them all out if you want to use them for all the chapters in this book.

attune
[ə tōōn', ə tyōōn']
v. to adjust; to bring into harmony

cinematography
[sin' ə mə tog' rə fē]
n. the art or technique of motion picture photography

connoisseur
[kon' ə sûr', -soor']
n. a person who can judge the best in an art or other field

disconcerted
[dis' kən sûrt' əd]
adj. disturbed; disordered; confused

epitomize
[i pit' ə mīz']
v. to serve as a typical or perfect example of; to typify

genre
[zhän' rə]
n. a class of artistic work (movie, book, etc.) having a particular form, content, or technique; a style

hail
[hāl]
v. 1. to approve enthusiastically
2. to cheer; to welcome; to call out to

juxtaposition
[juk' stə pə zish' ən]
n. an act of placing close together, especially for comparison or contrast

montage
[mon täzh']
n. 1. a film editing technique that presents images next to each other to convey an action, idea, or feeling
2. the combining of various elements to form a whole or single image

surreal
[sə rē' əl, -rēl']
adj. unreal; fantastic; having the quality of a dream

▊▊▊ WORDS TO WATCH

Which words would you like to practice with a bit more? Pick 3–5 words to study and list them below. Write the word, its definition, and compose your own sentence using the word correctly. This extra practice could be the final touch to learning a word.

	Word	Definition	Your Sentence
1.	_____	_____	_____
	_____	_____	_____
2.	_____	_____	_____
	_____	_____	_____
3.	_____	_____	_____
	_____	_____	_____
4.	_____	_____	_____
	_____	_____	_____
5.	_____	_____	_____
	_____	_____	_____

2 Music

Changing Sounds

Welcome to tonight's event! The Rolling Rock Show is designed to share fifty years of rock history in one night with over twenty performers on stage playing the songs you love.

Since its **inception** in the 1950s, rock 'n' roll has stirred
5 controversy. Elvis Presley and his swiveling hips startled many conservative Americans. They referred to rock 'n' roll as a **cacophony** and **censured** its being played on the radio or sold in record stores. But the "noise" could not be stopped or the movement quieted. Over the next few years rock 'n' roll
10 continued to break down the **decorum** of the young as crowds of women chased after the Beatles, screamed through their songs, and fainted at their concerts. During the 1960s, the young **clamored** for even more energetic music. The **execution** of rock music continued to change as rock venues grew. Performers
15 learned to **modulate** their voices and performances depending on whether they were singing in front of thousands at a concert like Woodstock or before an intimate group at a folk café. Performers like Jimi Hendrix and Janis Joplin showed how instruments and voices could be used in dynamic ways.

20 The complaints against rock music seemed barely **audible** by the mid-1970s when punk rock and the Sex Pistols broke the peace. High energy was again vital to the music scene, and poor **acoustics,** found in many of the small halls punk bands first played in, hardly seemed to matter to audiences that spent the
25 night pogoing and slam dancing. Music continued to evolve, and the 1980s and '90s embraced a variety of styles including new wave, hip-hop, and rap. For many performers today, it isn't unusual for their **repertoire** to include a classic song (like "Heatwave") from one of the '60s girl groups to a heavy-metal
30 inspired number.

Tonight's concert brings artists together from the 1950s to the present to perform songs from some of their most popular albums as well as works by other rock greats. Enjoy the fun, the flair, and the flavors of rock 'n' roll!

PREDICTING

For each set, write the definition on the line next to the word to which it belongs. If you are unsure, return to the reading on page 16, and underline any context clues you find. After you've made your predictions, check your answers against the Word List on page 21. Place a checkmark in the box next to each word whose definition you missed. These are the words you'll want to study closely.

SET ONE

a harsh sound	dignified conduct	the act of beginning	stated noisily	criticized in a harsh manner

- [ ] 1. **inception** (line 4) _____
- [ ] 2. **cacophony** (line 7) _____
- [ ] 3. **censured** (line 7) _____
- [ ] 4. **decorum** (line 10) _____
- [ ] 5. **clamored** (line 13) _____

SET TWO

all the works that a performer is prepared to present	a style of performance	to adjust
the features of a room that determine the quality of sounds in it	capable of being heard	

- [ ] 6. **execution** (line 13) _____
- [ ] 7. **modulate** (line 15) _____
- [ ] 8. **audible** (line 20) _____
- [ ] 9. **acoustics** (line 23) _____
- [ ] 10. **repertoire** (line 28) _____

SELF-TESTS

1 Circle the word that best completes each sentence.

1. The (cacophony, acoustics) in the concert hall were so good I could hear the characters when they whispered.

2. The performer's (execution, repertoire) surprised me. Not only could he sing and dance, but he could do magic and tell jokes.

3. The soft voice on the phone was scarcely (audible, modulate), but I thought it was my three-year-old niece who answered.

4. The gymnast's (clamor, execution) on the balance beam was flawless.

5. As the clapping increased or decreased, the candidate knew just how to (modulate, censure) her voice for the best effect.

6. At its (inception, repertoire) the mural looked like it would confront government policies, but people were amazed by the completed piece when the artist dared to put the president's head on the body of a pig.

7. The executive board voted to (modulate, censure) the treasurer for failing to keep receipts for all of his expenses last year.

8. The crowd (clamored, censured) for an encore, and the band obliged by playing three more songs.

9. The (decorum, execution) at the luncheon was disturbed when the waiter dropped a tray of sandwiches in the lap of noble Lady Windermere, thus causing the other women to giggle.

10. Someone had played with my radio, and I awoke to a (decorum, cacophony) of static, which upset my morning.

2 For each set, write the letter of the most logical analogy. See Completing Analogies on page 6 for instructions and practice.

SET ONE

_____ 1. modulate : voice ::   a. decorum : rudeness

_____ 2. lecture : classroom ::   b. sprain : ankle

_____ 3. inception : start ::   c. execution : boring

_____ 4. early : late ::   d. shy : modest

_____ 5. taste : salty ::   e. censure : Senate meeting

SET TWO

_____ 6. audible : silent ::   f. difficult : hard

_____ 7. fire : burns ::   g. brave : cowardly

_____ 8. water : pool ::   h. a car crash : cacophony

_____ 9. clamor : noise ::   i. book : chapters

_____ 10. pianist : repertoire ::   j. acoustics : auditorium

3 Finish the stories using the vocabulary words. Use each word once.

SET ONE

I was disappointed by the concert. First, the (1)_____ were so bad I couldn't hear the music. Then the management fiddled with the sound system, and the (2)_____ that emitted from the speakers caused the audience to cover its ears. Finally, even when the music was (3)_____ and not terrifying, we still weren't pleased. The new problem was the band's (4)_____. It turned out they had only five original songs, and they kept playing them over and over. The audience raised such a(n) (5)_____ about the poor quality of the whole evening that the owners eventually gave us back our money.

SET TWO

VOCABULARY LIST

| censure | modulate | execution | inception | decorum |

At the (6)_____ of rehearsals, the director told the singer to be bold in her performance of the gypsy. He said that (7)_____ was not appropriate. She was supposed to be a wild gypsy; dignified behavior did not fit the role. As rehearsals continued, the director told her that he did not mean to (8)_____ her whole performance, just the scene where she faces her lover's betrayal. She needed to (9)_____ her voice from soft and sad to an almost wild scream. Her (10)_____ of the piece would help to define her character's actions later in the opera.

WORD WISE

Collaborative Activity: Motivating with Music

If you are musically inclined, select some of your favorite pieces of music and get together with a few classmates to see how music can aid in learning. As you listen to the music, write five sentences with each using a vocabulary word that the music inspires, or write a story that the music inspires including five or six of the words to be studied in your story. Classical music works well, but music related to a chapter may also serve as inspiration and possibly as a memory aid. A few ideas include using music from *Wild Strawberries* or *Psycho* for relating to Chapter 1; The Beatles, Jimi Hendrix, or a punk band to relate to Chapter 2; music from Cambodia for Chapter 12; and music in a foreign language for Chapter 18. The ideas for the sentences or story may come from the tone of the music or the thoughts expressed in a song's lyrics. Share your sentences or stories with each other, and discuss the ideas the music brought out in relation to the words.

Write your own program notes. Pick a type of music or a performer and let the audience know what to expect from the show. Include at least seven of the vocabulary words in your write-up.

Some styles of music to choose from:

Rock   Country & Western   Rap   Blues   Hip-Hop   Alternative

_____

_____

_____

_____

_____

_____

_____

_____

_____

_____

_____

HINT

Generating Ideas

When you begin a writing project, it is usually helpful to get as many ideas as you can. Here are a few prewriting techniques to help the ideas flow:

Freewrite: Continuously write about your topic for five to ten minutes. Don't stop to correct any mistakes in spelling or other grammar areas. Write down anything that comes to your mind.

Brainstorm: Put your topic at the top of a piece of paper. Under the heading, list words or phrases that come to you about the topic. Even if an idea sounds silly put it down; it might lead to your best idea.

Cluster: Put your topic in the middle of a piece of paper and circle it. Use lines and circles to connect your ideas to the main topic and to put related ideas into groups or clusters. The finished project often looks like a spider web.

acoustics
[ə k oo' stiks]

n. the features of a room or auditorium that determine the quality of the sounds in it

audible
[ô' də bəl]

adj. capable of being heard; loud enough to hear

cacophony
[kə kof' ə nē]

n. a harsh, jarring sound

censure
[sen' shər]

v. to criticize in a harsh manner
n. 1. a strong expression of disapproval
   2. an official reprimand

clamor
[klam' ər]

v. to state noisily
n. a loud uproar; a loud and continued noise

decorum
[di kôr' əm, -kōr'-]

n. dignified conduct or appearance

execution
[ek' si kyoo' shən]

n. 1. a style of performance; technical skill, as in music
   2. the act of doing or performing
   3. the use of capital punishment

inception
[in sep' shən]

n. the act of beginning; a start

modulate
[moj' ə lāt']

v. to alter (the voice) according to circumstances; to adjust

repertoire
[rep' ər twär', -twôr', rep' ə-]

n. 1. all the works that a performer is prepared to present
   2. the skills used in a particular occupation

WORDS TO WATCH

Which words would you like to practice with a bit more? Pick 3–5 words to study and list them below. Write the word, its definition, and compose your own sentence using the word correctly. This extra practice could be the final touch to learning a word.

	Word	Definition	Your Sentence
1.			
2.			
3.			
4.			
5.			

More Than Numbers

Memo

To: Lucy
From: Kris
Date: Feb. 28, 2007
Re: Spring Window Display

5 It's time to design the spring window display. As you have a **finite** space to work with, you'll want to plan carefully. You will have the southwest window, which measures approximately 9' x 4' x 7'. The company envisions a **symmetrical** design showing women's fashions on one side and men's on the other with the same number of
10 mannequins arranged in similar positions on each side. We believe it is a **fallacy** of the fashion world that men's fashions aren't important. We want both genders to be given equal space and attention in the display. We would like a **gradation** of pastel colors in the background going from a dark blue to a pale pink. To separate the
15 men's and women's fashions, we want a row of rabbits to **bisect** the display case. The accompanying photos will give you an idea of what we want, but feel free to use your imagination. We trust that these guidelines will aid you in planning a display that captures the energy of spring and the new, colorful fashion line.

MEMORANDUM

20 May 6, 2007

Alexander,

I've compiled some **statistics** and found that our production levels were below **quota** for the first quarter. The usual allowance is 500 units, but in the **interval** between January 1 and April 1 there was a 20% drop in
25 output. Several **variables** could have caused the low numbers: the bad weather this winter, the flu that hit 40% of our workers, or that breakdown that took out 25% of our equipment for over a week. However, what I find to be the real **enigma** is why
30 production jumped up 100% from March to April. I am certainly puzzled about what is going on over there. Send me a memo giving me your take on the situation.

Toni

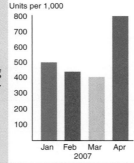

PREDICTING

For each set, write the definition on the line next to the word to which it belongs. If you are unsure, return to the reading on page 22, and underline any context clues you find. After you've made your predictions, check your answers against the Word List on page 27. Place a checkmark in the box next to each word whose definition you missed. These are the words you'll want to study closely.

SET ONE

having limits	to divide into two equal parts	regular in arrangement of corresponding parts
the passing of one shade of color to another by small degrees		a misconception

❑ 1. **finite** (line 5) _____

❑ 2. **symmetrical** (line 8) _____

❑ 3. **fallacy** (line 11) _____

❑ 4. **gradation** (line 13) _____

❑ 5. **bisect** (line 15) _____

SET TWO

a part of a total amount	a time between events	a puzzling occurrence
numerical facts	things that change	

❑ 6. **statistics** (line 22) _____

❑ 7. **quota** (line 23) _____

❑ 8. **interval** (line 24) _____

❑ 9. **variables** (line 25) _____

❑ 10. **enigma** (line 29) _____

SELF-TESTS

1 Put a T for true or F for false next to each sentence.

_____ 1. Statistics can be manipulated.

_____ 2. A house has a finite amount of space.

_____ 3. The exact circumstances of John F. Kennedy's death are an enigma.

_____ 4. Having a small triangle on one side of a picture and five large circles on the other side would be a symmetrical arrangement.

_____ 5. The weather in the United States is rarely variable.

_____ 6. It is a fallacy that studying helps students learn.

_____ 7. A thirty-degree change in temperature in ten minutes is an example of gradation.

_____ 8. The interval between a job interview and being accepted or rejected can make a person nervous.

_____ 9. It could be difficult to fill one's quota of strawberries to be picked if the person stops to eat several every five minutes.

_____10. If you cut a cake in nine pieces, you have bisected it.

2 Complete each sentence using the vocabulary words. Use each word once.

VOCABULARY LIST

bisect	fallacies	gradation	quota	symmetrical
enigma	finite	intervals	statistics	variable

1. The most recent _____ show that enrollment is up 20% in all math classes this semester compared to the last two semesters.

2. Our study showed that people were more attracted to the display with the _____ design than to the one with the irregular pattern.

3. How the huge statues on Easter Island were transported from the quarry to various spots around the island still remains a(n)_____.

4. I have put my money in an account with a(n)_____ interest rate; some months I will make more and some months less.

5. The main road was designed to _____ the town, putting the business area on one side and the residential area on the other.

6. As soon as I got my _____ of donations for the auction, I quit asking. Even though it is for a worthy cause, I am not really comfortable asking businesses to contribute items.

7. The directions said to plant the seeds at regular _____. I hope I spaced them evenly.

8. Unfortunately, my house has a _____ space for bookshelves. I keep buying more books, but I have run out of places to put them neatly.

9. I took notes through each _____ of the experiment so I would have an accurate record of the changes.

10. My logic instructor decided to test our critical thinking skills by giving us a list of arguments and asking us to find the _____ in them.

3 Complete the following analogies. See Completing Analogies on page 6 for instructions and practice.

1. long : short :: infinite : _____
2. skyscrapers : tall :: interest rates : _____
3. old : elderly :: misconception : _____
4. boring : exciting :: unbalanced : _____
5. what is at the far reaches of the universe : _____ :: poodle : dog
6. portion : _____ :: silence : hush
7. hem : a skirt :: _____ : a circle
8. a half hour : _____ :: fog : weather
9. bright : shiny :: stages : _____
10. government : _____ :: cook : stove

WORD WISE

Collocations

I was *disconcerted by* Mel's suggestion that I wasn't telling the whole truth about what I had done over the weekend. (Chapter 1)

The kids *clamored for* more juice; they were thirsty after playing in the park. (Chapter 2)

Most of the crowd spent the *interval between* halves rushing to the snack bar for more food and drinks. (Chapter 3)

The nurse checked the patient at *regular intervals* to make sure her breathing was steady. (Chapter 3)

Word Pairs

Audible/Inaudible: Audible (Chapter 2) means "capable of being heard." Inaudible means "incapable of being heard." The music from the rock concert was audible ten blocks away. Tammy's voice was inaudible a foot away from me because the music was so loud.

Symmetrical/Asymmetrical: Symmetrical (Chapter 3) means "balanced." Asymmetrical means "unbalanced; irregular." The symmetrical building attracted people to its graceful design. The asymmetrical building shocked people and displeased several of them.

Connotations and Denotations

Quota (Chapter 3): denotation—"the number or percentage of people of a specified kind allowed into a group or institution." In recent years quota systems have upset people and *quota* has taken on a negative connotation for many people. How do you feel when you hear that a college or other organization must fulfill a quota for admitting people?

Where Did It Come From?

Hail (Chapter 1): comes from the Middle English phrase *waes haeil* "be healthy." The word *wassail,* a drink, also comes from this origin, and it is often drunk during times of well wishing in the December holidays. When a movie is hailed as great, there are well wishes there too. Hail means "to welcome; to call out to" and "to approve enthusiastically."

Following the example of the reading on page 22, pick another field that could use mathematical terms, and write a memo using six of the vocabulary words. Occupations that you might consider are construction, coaching, banking, and interior design.

Memo

To: _____

From: _____

Date: _____

Re: _____

_____

_____

_____

_____

_____

_____

_____

_____

HINT

Outlining

When writing, it helps to make an outline of your ideas. You can always change the outline if you get better ideas, but it is a good way to help you get organized at the beginning of a writing project.

Informal Outline

Write your thesis (your main point) at the top of the paper. In a few key words, list the three or more points you want to cover.

1. _____

2. _____

3. _____

Look at the order in which you listed your points. Is there a reason to list them that way? Some possible methods of arrangement:

- Chronological (by time)
- From the least- to the most-important point
- From the most- to the least-important point
- A problem and its solution

Rearrange your points if you need to.

Now you will have an easier time as you start writing, and you won't forget an important point that you wanted to make.

▮▮▮▮ WORD LIST

bisect
[bī sekt', bī' sekt]
   v. 1. to divide into two equal or almost equal parts
   2. to intersect or cross

enigma
[ə nig' mə]
   n. a puzzling occurrence or person; a riddle

fallacy
[fal' ə sē]
   n. 1. a misconception; a misleading belief
   2. an unsound argument

finite
[fī' nīt]
   adj. having bounds or limits; measurable

gradation
[grā dā' shən]
   n. 1. the passing of one shade of color to another by small degrees
   2. change taking place through stages or gradually
   3. a stage in a series

interval
[in' tər vəl]
   n. 1. a time between events; a pause
   2. a space between things

quota
[kwō' tə]
   n. 1. a part of a total amount; an allotment; an allowance
   2. the number or percentage of people of a specified kind allowed into a group or institution

statistics
[stə tis' tiks]
   n. 1. (used with a plural v.) data; numerical facts
   2. (used with a singular v.) the science that deals with the study of numerical data

symmetrical
[si me' tri kəl]
   adj. regular in arrangement of corresponding parts; balanced

variable
[vâr' ē ə bəl]
   n. something that may or does change
   adj. changeable; inconstant

▮▮▮▮ WORDS TO WATCH

Which words would you like to practice with a bit more? Pick 3–5 words to study and list them below. Write the word, its definition, and compose your own sentence using the word correctly. This extra practice could be the final touch to learning a word.

	Word	Definition	Your Sentence
1.	_____	_____	_____
2.	_____	_____	_____
3.	_____	_____	_____
4.	_____	_____	_____
5.	_____	_____	_____

Challenges Faced

Before the United States became a
country, immigration was a part of the
American experience. Tired of being
persecuted for their religious beliefs,
5 the Pilgrims set sail from Plymouth,
England, in 1620. They did not seek
martyrdom by leaving England to settle
in the New World, just the opportunity
to freely practice their religion. The 101
10 passengers faced being **destitute** as they
left in September with two months of
rough seas before them and arrival in a
rugged, barely charted land as winter
approached. Still, like future
15 immigrants, they felt the challenges

were worth the rewards. They took animals and seed to start a new colony, and despite many
hardships, they survived. A new country was set in motion, and settlers steadily continued arriving.

The nineteenth century was to see a period of mass migration. In 1846 the potato crop began to
fail in Ireland and economic and political problems hit other European countries. Many Europeans
20 saw America as a place for **autonomy.** There they believed they would be free to start their own
businesses or farms and make their own religious and political decisions. Of course, many did not
come without **ambivalence.** It was difficult to leave family, friends, and a way of life they had known
for years. It was political oppression, starvation, and a hope for
a better future for themselves and their children that **induced**
25 most people to come to America. Records show close to 24
million people arrived in the United States between 1880 and
1920. An immigration period of such **magnitude** has not been
repeated in the United States.

Most immigrants have done their **utmost** to find a place in
30 American society. Balancing a respect for their original
country with their new homes has not always been easy.
Maybe one of the hardest aspects has been **placating** the
second and third generations who have not always understood
the traditions of their parents and grandparents as they try to fit
35 into American life. Many young people wonder why they must
wear traditional clothing to celebrate holidays whose
significance they don't really understand or why they must eat
traditional foods when they want hamburgers and French fries.
But these conflicts tend to resolve themselves with time as
40 families **ascertain** how to combine customs from the old
country with new ones from America to form a multicultural
society, taking the best from the many lands that make up this New World.

PREDICTING

For each set, write the definition on the line next to the word to which it belongs. If you are unsure, return to the reading on page 28, and underline any context clues you find. After you've made your predictions, check your answers against the Word List on page 33. Place a checkmark in the box next to each word whose definition you missed. These are the words you'll want to study closely.

SET ONE

poor	having conflicting feelings	harassed	extreme suffering	independence

❏ 1. **persecuted** (line 4) _____

❏ 2. **martyrdom** (line 7) _____

❏ 3. **destitute** (line 10) _____

❏ 4. **autonomy** (line 20) _____

❏ 5. **ambivalence** (line 22) _____

SET TWO

maximum	persuaded	calming
to find out definitely	greatness in significance, size, or rank	

❏ 6. **induced** (line 24) _____

❏ 7. **magnitude** (line 27) _____

❏ 8. **utmost** (line 29) _____

❏ 9. **placating** (line 32) _____

❏ 10. **ascertain** (line 40) _____

SELF-TESTS

1 Use the vocabulary words to complete the following analogies. For instructions, see Completing Analogies on page 6.

VOCABULARY LIST

induce	persecute	destitute	martyrdom	ascertain
placate	utmost	magnitude	autonomy	ambivalence

1. soft : hard :: anger : _____

2. death : _____ :: packing : taking a trip

3. confused : disturbed :: _____ : poor

4. _____ : least :: fresh : stale

5. an interview : nervousness :: going away to college : _____

6. _____ : the truth :: catch : a train

7. performer : audience :: teenager : _____

8. hang : a painting :: _____ : labor

9. harass : _____ :: gentle : meek

10. feather : light :: The Great Barrier Reef : _____

2 Finish these historical headlines. Use each word once.

VOCABULARY LIST

autonomy	placated	magnitude	persecuted	ambivalence
destitute	utmost	ascertain	induced	martyrdom

1. _____ of the American People Ends: Boston Tea Party Shows British What We Think of Taxation Without Representation (1773)

2. The _____ of the West Is "Amazing," Report Lewis and Clark (1806)

3. *President Lincoln Tries His _____ to Keep the Union Together (1860)*

4. _____ Indians Fight Back at Little Bighorn (1876)

5. San Francisco Earthquake Leaves Citizens _____ (1906)

6. Man Jumps to His Death! Suicide _____ by Stock Market Crash (1929)

7. *Americans _____ Hitler's Goal as World Domination: U.S. Enters the War! (1941)*

8. *Bra Burnings Said to Symbolize Women's _____ (1968)*

9. *The American People Won't Be _____ : President Nixon Must Go! (1974)*

10. Cell Phones and Computers—Greater Reliance on Technology Leads to _____ in Americans (2000)

3 Match the historical event to the rest of the sentence that completes the idea about the event's significance. You may need to do some research or consult a dictionary.

_____ 1. Landing on the moon

_____ 2. The Great Depression

_____ 3. The Civil War

_____ 4. The Declaration of Independence

_____ 5. The Salem witch trials

_____ 6. The discovery of gold at Sutter's Fort

_____ 7. The invention of the automobile

_____ 8. The Nineteenth Amendment

_____ 9. Prohibition

_____ 10. Building the Panama Canal

a. has created feelings of ambivalence depending on whether one is stuck in gridlock or enjoying the open road.

b. was fought because the South wanted autonomy.

c. led to martyrdom for those who would not admit to powers they didn't have or acts they didn't do.

d. left millions of people destitute.

e. was of the utmost concern because it took a ship two months to sail from the Pacific Ocean to the Atlantic Ocean during the Spanish-American War.

f. was a document of such magnitude that it led to the formation of a new country.

g. tried to placate concerns about the evils of drinking.

h. helped scientists ascertain what it is made of.

i. gave women the right to vote, ending years of persecution.

j. induced money-hungry people to head to California.

WORD WISE

Internet Activity: How Often Is It Used?

Here is an activity that will illustrate different contexts for the vocabulary words and emphasize the enormity of the Internet. Type a vocabulary word into a search engine such as Google or Yahoo. See how many times the word is found. Read through the first entries and see how the word is used. Find a Web site that seems interesting. Open it and look for the word again to see it in its full context. For example, the word _connoisseur_ turned up 3,320,000 results. Among the first ten entries it was used in the contexts of Connoisseur Boating Holidays, Caribbean Connoisseur, New Music Connoisseur, and The Low Carb Connoisseur. Sometimes you will get a lot more results. _Thesis_ turned up 76,400,000 results. You can also be surprised at how a word is used. Results for some other vocabulary words turned up the names of societies and magazine titles. Have fun seeing what is out there. Share your finds with classmates. What words did people pick to look up? Which word had the least results and which the most? Did anyone find an exciting site?

Your word: _____

Number of results: _____

A sample context: _____

Name of the Web site you visited: _____

Answer the following questions dealing with U.S. history.

1. Name two groups that have been persecuted. _____
   _____

2. Name two situations that have induced people to fight for changes in laws.
   _____   _____

3. The magnitude of the car's influence on American life continues to this day. Give three examples
   of its effects. _____
   _____

4. What are two kinds of autonomy people have fought for?
   _____   _____

5. Name an event that you think must have caused ambivalence in some people.
   _____

6. Name two events that have made people destitute.
   _____   _____

7. What are two possible actions the government can take to placate angry citizens?
   _____   _____

8. Which invention do you think has had the utmost influence on society? Why?
   _____
   _____

9. Name two ways you could ascertain which candidate you should vote for in the next mayoral
   election.
   _____   _____

10. What two beliefs might a person hold that could lead to martyrdom?
    _____   _____

HINT

Multiple Meanings

Most words have more than one meaning. For some words one meaning is used more often than the others, but for other words two or three of their meanings are equally well used. For example, a bat is "a wooden club used to hit a ball" or "a mammal that flies, usually at night." Both meanings for bat are frequently used. However, among the meanings for *cure* as a noun, most people would know "a means of healing" and possibly "a process of preserving meat, fish, etc. by smoking, salting, or the like," but the meaning of "the office or district of a curate or parish priest" is not seen as often. This book usually gives alternate meanings as long as they are fairly common. One meaning will be used in the reading for the chapter, but the Self-Tests that follow the reading may use the additional meanings, so carefully look over the Word List before you start the Self-Tests. If you ever see a word used in a way you are not familiar with, check a dictionary to see if it has another meaning you do not know. You may be surprised at how many meanings even a short and seemingly simple word may have. *Webster's Collegiate Dictionary* lists twenty-four meanings for the word *so*. Just be prepared for the fun and challenges that multiple meanings provide.

WORD LIST

ambivalence
[am biv′ ə ləns]
n. having conflicting feelings, such as love and hate, about a person, object, or idea

ascertain
[as′ ər tān′]
v. to find out definitely; to learn with certainty

autonomy
[ô ton′ ə mē]
n. independence; the quality of being self-governing

destitute
[des′ tə to͞ot′]
adj. devoid; poor; impoverished

induce
[in do͞os′]
v. 1. to persuade; to cause
2. to infer by inductive reasoning

magnitude
[mag′ ni to͞od′]
n. greatness in significance, size, or rank

martyrdom
[mär′ tər dəm]
n. 1. extreme suffering
2. the state of being a martyr (one who chooses death or makes a sacrifice rather than give up religious faith or other belief)

persecute
[pûr′ sə kyo͞ot′]
v. to harass; to annoy continuously

placate
[plā′ kāt′, plak′ āt′]
v. to pacify; to calm

utmost
[ut′ mōst′]
n. the greatest amount or level; maximum
adj. most extreme; of the greatest degree

WORDS TO WATCH

Which words would you like to practice with a bit more? Pick 3–5 words to study and list them below. Write the word, its definition, and compose your own sentence using the word correctly. This extra practice could be the final touch to learning a word.

Word	Definition	Your Sentence
1. _____	_____	_____
_____	_____	_____
2. _____	_____	_____
_____	_____	_____
3. _____	_____	_____
_____	_____	_____
4. _____	_____	_____
_____	_____	_____
5. _____	_____	_____
_____	_____	_____

5 Word Parts I

Look for words with these **prefixes, roots,** and/or **suffixes** as you work through this book. You may have already seen some of them, and you will see others in later chapters. Learning basic word parts can help you figure out the meanings of unfamiliar words.

prefix: a word part added to the beginning of a word that changes the meaning of the root
root: a word's basic part with its essential meaning
suffix: a word part added to the end of a word; indicates the part of speech

WORD PART	MEANING	EXAMPLES AND DEFINITIONS
Prefixes		
ambi-, amphi-	both, around	*ambivalence:* having conflicting feelings; feeling both ways *amphitheater:* a round structure with seats rising from an open space
epi-	after, upon	*epilogue:* a speech after a play; material at the end of a book *epidermis:* the outermost layer of the skin; upon the surface
mag-	great, large	*magnitude:* greatness *magnify:* to make larger
post-	after, behind	*posterity:* future generations *postdoctoral:* pertaining to study done after receiving a doctorate
Roots		
-duc-	to lead	*conducive:* leading toward *induce:* lead one to do
-grad-, -gress-	to step	*retrograde:* to step backward; to retire or retreat *transgress:* to step across a limit; to violate
-lev-	lift, light, rise	*alleviate:* to lighten; to reduce *elevator:* a device that lifts people
-pon-, -pos-	to put, to place	*proponent:* one who puts one's point forward *juxtaposition:* an act of placing close together
-rog-	to ask	*prerogative:* a special right to ask for something *interrogate:* to ask questions

Suffixes

-dom (makes a noun)	state or quality of	*martyrdom:* the state of suffering *freedom:* the quality of being free
-eur (makes a noun)	one who	*connoisseur:* a person who can judge the best in an art or other field *entrepreneur:* a person who assumes the risks of a business
-tude (makes a noun)	state or quality of	*magnitude:* the quality of being great *gratitude:* state of being thankful

SELF-TESTS

1 Read each definition and choose the appropriate word. Use each word once. The meaning of the word part is underlined to help you make the connection. Refer to the Word Parts list if you need help.

VOCABULARY LIST

chauffeur	gradual	ambidextrous	levitate	postbellum
wisdom	conductor	deposit	prerogative	magnum

1. capable of using <u>both</u> hands_____
2. occurring <u>after</u> a war_____
3. the person who <u>leads</u> the orchestra _____
4. <u>to put</u> money in the bank _____
5. a special right <u>to ask</u> for something _____
6. <u>one who</u> drives a car for a living _____
7. a <u>large</u> wine bottle _____
8. changing by small degrees or <u>step-by-step</u> _____
9. <u>the quality of</u> being intelligent _____
10. to float or <u>lift</u> a person or thing _____

2 Finish the sentences with the meaning of each word part. Use each meaning once. The word part is underlined to help you make the connection.

VOCABULARY LIST

after	great	lead	step	rise
upon	put	ask	state	around

1. She received a <u>post</u>humous award: it was given to her the year _____ she died.
2. My free<u>dom</u> is important to me. It is a(n) _____ that I don't take for granted.
3. I moved the <u>lev</u>er to make the door _____.

4. The police interrogated the man for two hours; they had a lot of questions to _____.

5. My friends tried to seduce me into going to the movies, but they couldn't _____ me astray; I stayed home and studied.

6. His answers were ambiguous: he kept dancing _____ my questions.

7. I transposed the numbers on my check: I _____ the "1" before the "2" and ended up being nine dollars short.

8. Their house is magnificent; everything about it is _____.

9. When I graduate from college, I will be one _____ closer to being an independent woman.

10. The epitaph _____ his tomb told about how much he loved his family.

3 Finish the story using the word parts below. Use each word part once. Your knowledge of word parts, as well as the context clues, will help you create the correct words. If you do not understand the meaning of a word you have made, check the dictionary for the definition or to see whether the word exists.

WORD PARTS LIST

lev	ambi	epi	mag	duc
tude	gress	pos	rog	dom

THE SPACE VOYAGE

Katy was suffering from bore(1)_____, until

she met the aliens. She was ab(2)_____ted by

the aliens and taken onto their spacecraft. They told her

about the (3)_____nitude of their mission.

They had to repopulate their planet, and they asked her

to be a sur(4)_____ate mother for a short time

as there were not enough female beings on their planet.

Katy hated to hurt the pro(5)_____ of another

planet and she thought this adventure might be exciting,

so she agreed to accompany them. The creatures were

(6)_____guous about how far they had to travel

on the ship. They said time didn't have any

re(7)_____ance in their world.

  Katy enjoyed visiting with the aliens. They were the (8)_____tome of kindness. They

continually showed their grati(9)_____ by bringing her gifts and her favorite foods. Still she

began to miss her family and friends. The aliens were quick to sense her restlessness, and they put

Katy on a spaceship home. The trip had helped to dis(10)_____e of the dreariness in Katy's

life; she was satisfied to be back on Earth.

4 Pick the best definition for each underlined word using your knowledge of word parts. Circle the word part in each of the underlined words.

a. the quality of being complete

b. a person who puts one's point forward

c. one who provides massage as a job

d. disease spread upon many people

e. able to operate on both land and water

f. showing a great spirit

g. a raised area of earth along a river

h. to lead or bring in

i. claiming superior rights

j. examination of a body after death

_____ 1. The masseur had strong hands.

_____ 2. The levee wasn't high enough to keep the water from flooding the houses.

_____ 3. The postmortem revealed that the man had been poisoned.

_____ 4. The arrogant man demanded everything done his way.

_____ 5. The magnanimous donation helped us build the hospital sooner than we expected.

_____ 6. The epidemic almost wiped out the small village.

_____ 7. The navy found that amphibious vehicles were best suited for the mission.

_____ 8. Four years after his retirement, the community decided it was time to induct Phillips into the local Sports Hall of Fame.

_____ 9. We have a plentitude of food for dinner with the pizza I got and the chicken you brought.

_____ 10. She was a proponent of the new park from the beginning; she continually let people know that the neighborhood kids needed a safe place to play.

5 A good way to remember word parts is to pick one word that uses a word part and understand how that word part functions in the word. Then you can apply that meaning to other words that have the same word part. Use the words to help you match the word part to its meaning.

SET ONE

_____ 1. **ambi-, amphi-:** ambiguous, ambivalent, amphibious

_____ 2. **mag-:** magnificent, magnify, magnitude

_____ 3. **-dom:** martydom, freedom, wisdom

_____ 4. **-duc-:** induce, conductor, seduce

_____ 5. **-eur:** entrepreneur, masseur, connoisseur

a. one who

b. to lead

c. state or quality of

d. both, around

e. great, large

SET TWO

_____ 6. **-pon-, -pos-:** proponent, juxtaposition, deposit

_____ 7. **-lev-:** levity, levitate, elevator

_____ 8. **-grad-, -gress-:** gradual, gradation, transgress

_____ 9. **-rog-:** interrogate, derogatory, arrogant

_____ 10. **-tude:** magnitude, gratitude, aptitude

f. lift, light, rise

g. state or quality of

h. to step

i. to put, to place

j. to ask

WORD WISE

This lesson uses antonyms—words that mean the opposite of the unknown word—as the clues. In the paragraph below, circle the antonyms you find for the underlined words. Then, on the lines that follow the paragraph, write a word that is the opposite of the antonym as your definition of the word.

When I went to visit, Marsha's greeting was cordial. A few people had told me that she was often cold and unfriendly, but I did not find her so. We merrily chatted for an hour, when suddenly she cast an aspersion on my blouse. I thought she was going to compliment it when she mentioned the unusual color, but I was wrong. I was dejected. I had been so excited about making a new friend. What I had hoped to be the beginning of a new friendship turned out to be its demise.

Your Definition

1. Cordial _____

2. Aspersion _____

3. Dejected _____

4. Demise _____

INTERACTIVE EXERCISE

Use the dictionary to find a word you don't know that uses each word part listed below. Write the meaning of the word part, the word, and the definition. If your dictionary has the etymology (history) of the word, see how the word part relates to the meaning, and write the etymology after the definition.

Word Part	Meaning	Word	Definition and Etymology
EXAMPLE:			
mag-	great, large	magnifico	1. a Venetian nobleman
			2. any person of high rank. from
			Latin magnificus, magn(us)
			large, great
1. ambi-			
2. epi-			

3. *post-* _____

_____

_____

4. *-lev-* _____

_____

_____

5. *-grad-* _____

_____

_____

HINT

Etymologies

An etymology is the history of a word. Some dictionaries will explain in an entry how the word came into existence. Words can be developed in several ways such as being made up, coming from a person's name, or evolving from foreign languages. Reading a word's etymology can sometimes help you remember the meaning. For example, the word **dismal** comes from the Latin *dies mali. Dies* is the plural of day and *mali* the plural of evil. In Middle English the word meant unlucky days; there were two days in each month that were thought to be unfavorable. The word now means "causing depression or dread." It is easy to see how this definition came from the idea of unlucky days. Not all words have interesting histories, but taking the time to read an etymology can be useful. If you get excited about word origins, there are books available on the subject that show how fascinating language can be.

6 Computers

Technology Today

MATT: Thanks for talking to me, Dan; I am a computer **neophyte** and have so many questions about using the Internet. I'm afraid of committing some horrid **transgression** as I explore the Web. I hope I don't sound like an idiot. I had computerphobia for a long time, but computers have become so **ubiquitous**, I think I had better get used to them.

5 DAN: Don't worry. In computer **jargon** you're a newbie, and everyone's been a beginner at some point. I'll be happy to help : -). Let me go over a few **netiquette** points. When you are chatting, it is considered rude to **flame** people or make an angry or insulting remark. Writing in all capital letters looks like you are shouting and can be taken as flaming.

MATT: Thanks for the tip. I may have done that by accident. What does : -) mean after the word 10 "help"?

DAN: That is an **emoticon**, also known as a smiley. That one is a happy face. People use them to show their feelings. If I were sad, I might have written : - (.

MATT: Thanks : -) . If I want to use the Internet to find out about a particular subject, what should I do?

15 DAN: You can start by typing your interest and the word "**newsgroup**," such as "tennis newsgroup," into an Internet search engine like Yahoo! or Google, and you'll find a list of sites to check out. You can then join one of these newsgroups, which is just an online discussion group on a specific topic. When you first enter a discussion, take the time to read the Frequently Asked Question (FAQs) section and do some lurking so that you 20 don't ask questions that are likely to annoy the established users.

MATT: What is lurking?

DAN: Lurking is observing without participating. When you get a feel for a group, join in.

MATT: Are things I write on the Internet safe? Can anyone read my e-mail?

DAN: That depends on where you are posting material. If you are in a public discussion group, 25 people can read what you write. It is still uncertain who may have access to your e-mail. Although **encryption** has gotten better in recent years, especially as people send credit card information over the Internet, it is still a good idea to be cautious about the messages you write.

MATT: There is so much to learn. Do you think I will ever know it all?

30 DAN: I don't think anyone can. When the **prototype** for the modern computer was invented in the late 1940s, I don't think people really foresaw how many uses the computer would have. New words are coined daily in the computer field. Acronyms are especially important. In fact, I'll brb.

MATT: What does "brb" mean?

35 MATT: Dan, where are you?

▐▐▌▌▐ PREDICTING

For each set, write the definition on the line next to the word to which it belongs. If you are unsure, return to the reading on page 40, and underline any context clues you find. After you've made your predictions, check your answers against the Word List on page 45. Place a checkmark in the box next to each word whose definition you missed. These are the words you'll want to study closely.

SET ONE

online manners	violation of a law or command	beginner
the language of a particular profession or group		existing everywhere

- ❏ 1. **neophyte** (line 1) _____
- ❏ 2. **transgression** (line 2) _____
- ❏ 3. **ubiquitous** (line 4) _____
- ❏ 4. **jargon** (line 5) _____
- ❏ 5. **netiquette** (line 6) _____

SET TWO

an online discussion group	the model on which something is based	an online graphic
to insult or criticize online	a way of coding information	

- ❏ 6. **flame** (line 7) _____
- ❏ 7. **emoticon** (line 11) _____
- ❏ 8. **newsgroup** (line 15) _____
- ❏ 9. **encryption** (line 26) _____
- ❏ 10. **prototype** (line 30) _____

▐▐▌▌▐ SELF-TESTS

1 Circle the correct meaning of each vocabulary word.

1. flame:	to insult online	to compliment online
2. neophyte:	expert	beginner
3. transgression:	doing as commanded	violation of a law
4. jargon:	pretentious language	simple language
5. ubiquitous:	existing everywhere	found nowhere
6. netiquette:	bad habits	online manners
7. prototype:	a model	a silly example
8. encryption:	coding information	sharing information

9. newsgroup: online discussion group a weekly newsmagazine

10. emoticon: a word used to express an opinion a graphic that shows one's feelings

2 Match each vocabulary word to the appropriate situation or example. Use each word once.

VOCABULARY LIST

| neophyte | netiquette | encryption | prototype | flame |
| jargon | emoticon | newsgroup | transgression | ubiquitous |

1. ; -) (winking) _____

2. hard drive, software, CD-ROM, lol _____

3. YOU'RE SO STUPID; TEN PEOPLE ALREADY ASKED THAT QUESTION _____

4. .com _____

5. the first washing machine _____

6. on elementary education, on cars _____

7. unsure which button to push to minimize a program _____

8. reading the Frequently Asked Questions before you enter a discussion _____

9. posting your friend's secret on the Internet _____

10. #jf4^)6*9j _____

3 Complete the following sentences using the vocabulary words. Use each word once.

VOCABULARY LIST

| encryption | flaming | prototype | transgression | ubiquitous |
| jargon | newsgroup | emoticon | netiquette | neophyte |

1. I am a(n) _____ compared to my best friend who has been using computers for the last fifteen years.

2. To show my shock at Laura's e-mail announcement of her pregnancy, I used the _____ : - O.

3. I know it is considered rude, but I couldn't stop from _____ the person who kept making comments that were off-topic.

4. Now that I have been going to chat rooms for a few months, I understand how important _____ is. Just as in real life, there are rules to follow that make conversations run smoothly.

5. So much Internet _____ is based on acronyms that I'm often unsure of what someone is telling me.

6. Johnny committed a major _____ when he ate in front of the computer. He spilled cookie crumbs on the keyboard and got in trouble.

7. I was afraid to buy anything online because I thought my credit card number would be stolen, but I read about the _____ methods on a couple sites, and I have been successfully shopping electronically for months.

8. Computer terms have become so _____ that my five-year-old said he wanted an "e-hug" from me instead of a real hug.

9. The computer show featured a(n) _____ for a new computer that looked like a pencil.

10. After Ina's trip to Egypt, she joined a(n) _____ on archeology. She was really excited about sharing information on mummies and pyramids.

WORD WISE

Collocations

The *magnitude of the problem* unfolded as the day went on. One malfunction led to the creation of several other troubles. (Chapter 4)

This project is *of the utmost importance,* so I want you to devote all of your energy to it. (Chapter 4)

Connotations and Denotations

Martyrdom (Chapter 4): denotation—"the state of being a martyr (one who chooses death or makes a sacrifice rather than give up religious faith or other belief)." The connotation of martyrdom and martyr can take two forms. Many see martyrs as brave people who stand up for what they believe in. Others see a martyr as either a fool who won't make compromises to fit in or as a person who actually desires some kind of fame by choosing death. How do you view martyrdom? Is it a grand ideal or a crazy idea?

Where Did It Come From?

Jargon (Chapter 6): in the Middle Ages meant "twittering" and later "meaningless chatter." That meaning still applies to one of the definitions "unintelligible talk," and likely the definition—"the language of a particular profession or group"—sounded like meaningless chatter to those not involved in that profession.

Pretend you have joined a newsgroup on a subject that interests you, and write a posting using at least six of the vocabulary words.

HINT

Study Often

Don't try to fit all of your studying into one session before a test. Look at your notes for a class often. Review them the day you write them while the information is fresh in your mind in case you want to add some material. Do a weekly review of material so that as you learn new material you can build on the old information. These same ideas apply to learning vocabulary. Look often at the flash cards you make. Even taking ten minutes a day to go over the words for that week will help you remember the meanings. While you are waiting for another class to start, for a friend who is late, or for the bus to come, take some of that time to review the words.

emoticon
[i mō' ti kon']
n. a graphic made by combining punctuation marks and other characters to show one's feelings online

encryption
[en krip' shən]
n. a way of coding information in a file or e-mail message so that if it is intercepted as it travels over a network, it cannot be read

flame
[flām]
v. 1. to insult or criticize angrily online
2. to behave in an offensive manner online; to rant
n. an act of angry criticism online

jargon
[jär' gən, -gon]
n. 1. the language of a particular profession or group
2. unintelligible talk
3. pretentious language

neophyte
[nē' ə fīt']
n. a beginner or novice

netiquette
[net' i kit', -ket']
n. online manners or etiquette; an informal code of conduct for online behavior

newsgroup
[nōoz' grōop]
n. an online discussion group on a specific topic

prototype
[prō' tə tīp']
n. 1. the model on which something is based; a pattern
2. something that serves as a typical example of a group

transgression
[trans gresh' ən, tranz-]
n. violation of a law, duty, or command; the exceeding of limits

ubiquitous
[yōo bik' wi təs]
adj. existing or being everywhere, especially at the same time

▌▌▌▌ WORDS TO WATCH

Which words would you like to practice with a bit more? Pick 3–5 words to study and list them below. Write the word, its definition, and compose your own sentence using the word correctly. This extra practice could be the final touch to learning a word.

Word	Definition	Your Sentence
1. _____	_____	_____
	_____	_____
2. _____	_____	_____
	_____	_____
3. _____	_____	_____
	_____	_____
4. _____	_____	_____
	_____	_____
5. _____	_____	_____
	_____	_____

Greetings, All

Greetings are a **socialization** behavior that most people take for granted because greetings are so **pervasive** in society. But from a young age, people are taught the appropriate greetings for different circumstances.
5 Studying everyday life can help us better understand why we act the ways we do. Sociologist Erving Goffman points out that greetings are part of our face-to-face contacts, phone conversations, and letters. Two important areas that greetings illuminate are **status** and
10 cultural differences. For example, which person says "hello" first and how someone is greeted can be part of the **stratification** system in a society. In the past, a man removed his hat and bowed to greet a prince or king; this behavior showed his lower rank in the society. This
15 greeting became truncated over time. Later, people began to greet equals by just lifting the hat, and then by touching the hat. Finally, a motion toward the hat was enough of a greeting among friends.

     Greeting rules also vary by country. In France,
20 people kiss each other on the cheek as a friendly, everyday greeting, but this type of behavior is not the **norm** in the United States. Mahadev Apte explored another cultural difference in the use of "thank-you" forms in the South Asian languages of Hindi and Marathi. In these cultures, a "thank-you" form is
25 essential in public ceremonies and in introductions to books, but thank-yous are **taboo** with family members, close friends, or in business transactions. In some cultures, people may be **ostracized** for not following proper greeting behavior. In fact, knowing what is forbidden and accepted has become important in international business, as a mistake in greeting rituals can ruin a business deal or a company.
30   **Deviating** from **conventional** greeting behavior can lead to problems. For example, linguist C. A. Ferguson, as an informal experiment, didn't respond to his secretary's "good morning" for two days in a row. He reported that the atmosphere was unpleasant on the first day and tense on the second day. By the third day, to **alleviate** the stress and save their working relationship, he discontinued the experiment. Obviously, what people say and do in what may seem like simple everyday greetings can have more relevance than people imagine.

PREDICTING

For each set, write the definition on the line next to the word to which it belongs. If you are unsure, return to the reading on page 46, and underline any context clues you find. After you've made your predictions, check your answers against the Word List on page 51. Place a checkmark in the box next to each word whose definition you missed. These are the words you'll want to study closely.

SET ONE

social standing	a standard	the act of developing levels of class
a learning process	having the quality to spread	

- ☐ 1. **socialization** (line 1) _____
- ☐ 2. **pervasive** (line 2) _____
- ☐ 3. **status** (line 9) _____
- ☐ 4. **stratification** (line 12) _____
- ☐ 5. **norm** (line 22) _____

SET TWO

excluded	to relieve	a prohibition	moving away from	customary

- ☐ 6. **taboo** (line 25) _____
- ☐ 7. **ostracized** (line 26) _____
- ☐ 8. **deviating** (line 30) _____
- ☐ 9. **conventional** (line 30) _____
- ☐ 10. **alleviate** (line 33) _____

SELF-TESTS

1 Put a T for true or F for false next to each statement.

_____ 1. A group might consider ostracizing someone with an unpleasant odor.

_____ 2. Ox-drawn carts are pervasive in American society.

_____ 3. A massage can help to alleviate stress.

_____ 4. One's status in society is often determined by one's job.

_____ 5. Spending the weekend skiing in Switzerland is the norm for most students.

_____ 6. Riding a pogo stick is a conventional method of transportation.

_____ 7. Blowing bubbles with one's gum is considered taboo in the classroom.

_____ 8. There is no type of stratification in the military.

_____ 9. A flooded road can cause people to deviate from an intended route.

_____ 10. Socialization can take place at the dinner table.

2 Finish the reading using the vocabulary words. Use each word once.

VOCABULARY LIST				
alleviate	norm	pervasive	conventional	socialization
status	taboo	deviate	ostracized	stratification

FITTING IN

The years spent in school are certainly an important part of the (1)_____ process. It is during school hours that children learn how to get along with others and how different groups act. Certainly (2)_____ is part of the schoolyard. Some students are the "in" group and have special privileges, while others are considered "outsiders." One's (3)_____ in school can help determine whether one is invited to parties or teased during recess. Those who (4)_____ from the accepted standards, whether by wearing out-of-style clothes or not keeping up on the latest slang, can expect to be criticized. In extreme cases these students may even be (5)_____. What is considered right and wrong can change quickly. One week it may be (6)_____ to wear stripes, and the next week stripes can be all the rage.

To (7)_____ the stress of trying to fit in, parents should give their children love and encouragement at home. The need to fit in, however, is (8)_____ in society, so parents should balance accepting some requests for the latest gadgets with giving in to every childhood whim. What was the (9)_____ when parents went to school and what is the standard today can vary greatly, and parents must be willing to change their ideas of what is and isn't acceptable. The (10)_____ wisdom that "father knows best" may not always hold true in a rapidly changing world.

3 Circle the word that best completes each sentence.

1. Instead of using the (conventional, pervasive) entrance, my brother likes to enter the house through his bedroom window.

2. To (deviate, alleviate) the pain, Elizabeth put ice on her sore knee.

3. I kept asking about the (norm, status) of the flight, but no one at the check-in counter was sure when the plane would take off.

4. It is usually considered (taboo, norm) to ask how much money a person makes.

5. When no one got a raise, discontent was the (conventional, pervasive) mood in the office.

6. I enrolled my son in preschool to help his (socialization, stratification).

7. We had to (deviate, alleviate) from the syllabus because it was worthwhile to attend the assembly.

8. In some countries, such as India, (stratification, taboo) has been very important to how people are treated.

9. It is considered the (norm, taboo) to tip waiters in the United States, but that is not the custom in all countries.

10. Sarah was (ostracized, alleviated) from the cooking club when she brought in a peanut butter and jelly sandwich and called it gourmet food

WORD WISE

Collocations

The *conventional wisdom* has been that eating dessert will make a person fat, but it is more likely the portion size and type of dessert that will put on the pounds. (Chapter 7)

We had to *deviate from* the plan when Michelle called in sick since we only had three people to give the presentation instead of four. (Chapter 7)

The *socialization process* starts early with children learning what actions are and are not acceptable in their family. (Chapter 7)

Connotations and Denotations

Conventional (Chapter 7): denotation—"conforming to established standards." For some people the connotation of *conventional* is "boring." They think that "conforming to established standards" is old-fashioned, and they would rather try something new or different. When you hear the word *conventional,* how do you react?

Where Did It Come From?

Ostracize (Chapter 7): comes from the Greek *ostrakon* "tile or pottery." In ancient Greece when a city wanted to see if a person should be forced to leave because he was trouble for the state, a vote was taken on tiles, and if six thousand people voted "yes," the person was banished for a minimum of five years. Today ostracize has the same effect "to exclude, by general consent, from society or from privileges," but without the voting tiles.

Taboo (Chapter 7): comes from the Tongan word *tabu* "marked as holy." Tongan is a Polynesian language spoken in the Tonga island group, which is located in the southern Pacific Ocean. Taboos were originally restrictions against mentioning certain matters in fear that they might anger the gods. The word came to mean "a prohibition excluding something from use or mention." What is considered taboo changes depending on the society and the time period.

INTERACTIVE EXERCISE

Give two examples for each of the following.

1. Where can you see socialization taking place?

   _____   _____

2. What are pervasive problems in today's society?

   _____   _____

3. What jobs have a high status in American society?

   _____   _____

4. What institutions use stratification?

   _____   _____

5. What situations might cause someone to deviate from his or her regular behavior?

   _____   _____

6. What norms are found in the classroom?

   _____   _____

7. What topics are usually considered taboo at dinner parties?

   _____   _____

8. Why might someone be ostracized from a group?

   _____   _____

9. What are conventional Mother's Day gifts?

   _____   _____

10. What do you do to alleviate pain when you are sick?

   _____   _____

HINT

Finding a Place to Study

To concentrate on what you are studying, you need to find the right environment for you. Because most people concentrate better in a quiet space, try turning off the television and radio and see if you can better focus on your work. Also look for a place with good light; you don't want to strain your eyes. You should be comfortable, so find a chair you like, or if you need to take notes, sit at a table. For some people, sitting outside in a park or the backyard provides a pleasant and productive place to read. See what works best for you depending on what you are studying. Change your environment if you can't focus.

alleviate
[ə lē′ vē āt′]
v. to relieve; to reduce

conventional
[kən ven′ shən əl]
adj. 1. customary
2. conforming to established standards

deviate
[dē′ vē āt′]
v. 1. to move away from a norm or set behavior
2. to cause to turn aside or to differ

norm
[nôrm]
n. a standard or pattern regarded as typical for a specific group

ostracize
[os′ trə siz′]
v. to exclude, by general consent, from society or from privileges

pervasive
[pər vā′ siv, -ziv]
adj. having the quality to spread throughout or permeate

socialization
[so′ shə li zā′ shən]
n. the process whereby an individual learns the values and behaviors appropriate to his or her culture and social standing

status
[stā′ təs, stat′ əs]
n. 1. a relative position; standing, especially social standing
2. high standing
3. situation

stratification
[strat′ ə fi kā′ shən]
n. the act or process of developing levels of class or privilege

taboo
[tə boo′, ta-]
n. a prohibition excluding something from use or mention
v. to exclude from use

WORDS TO WATCH

Which words would you like to practice with a bit more? Pick 3–5 words to study and list them below. Write the word, its definition, and compose your own sentence using the word correctly. This extra practice could be the final touch to learning a word.

Word	Definition	Your Sentence
1. _____	_____	_____
2. _____	_____	_____
3. _____	_____	_____
4. _____	_____	_____
5. _____	_____	_____

8 Composition

Exploring an Issue

Community Research Project

First Draft Due: April 8

Final Draft Due: May 1

5 Your assignment is to pick a problem in the community and research ways to resolve it. For example, you might study the need for more parking downtown, how to deal with freeway traffic, or how to improve the county recycling program. There are numerous areas to explore.

10 • Make your **thesis** clear in the first paragraph of your paper. Readers should understand the point you want to make.

• Add a **refutation** section to your paper. Look at other sides of the issue and show how your plan is better than theirs.

• Your **intention** is to help the community by noting the problem and presenting a valid
15 solution.

In writing the paper, remember the important concepts we have covered this semester.

• **coherence**: all the examples in your paper should relate to your thesis.

• **diction**: your choice of words should reflect your purpose and knowledge of your audience. Remember this is a formal paper. Be aware of the **denotations** (dictionary definitions) and
20 **connotations** (the feelings and emotions words take on) of the words you use. The different meanings will influence your readers.

• **transitions**: transitions help your writing flow. You can use transition words, such as *however*, *then*, *next*, and *first* (see your writing text for more examples), repeat key words, or use **parallelism**. Remember that putting lists in the same structure makes your writing flow.
25 (Examples: My hobbies are reading, writing, and swimming; I like to read, to write, and to swim).

• Include at least three quotations and three **paraphrases** in the proper format as discussed in class. Remember to put the page number where you found the quote in parentheses.

30 Quotation: use the writer's own words and put the words in quotation marks.

Example: E. M. Forster states, "Property makes its owner feel that he ought to do something to it" (64).

Paraphrase: put the writer's words into your own words and do not use quotation marks.

Example: In writing about buying some woodland, E. M. Forster feels that one of the effects
35 the land has on him is making him want to change it in some way (64).

As you write the paper, have fun finding out about the community and helping to solve one of its problems.

▮▮▮▮▮ PREDICTING

For each set, write the definition on the line next to the word to which it belongs. If you are unsure, return to the reading on page 52, and underline any context clues you find. After you've made your predictions, check your answers against the Word List on page 57. Place a checkmark in the box next to each word whose definition you missed. These are the words you'll want to study closely.

SET ONE

the act of disproving a statement	the choice and use of words	a plan
the act of disproving a statement	the choice and use of words	a plan
a proposal that is defended by argument	consistency	

❏ 1. **thesis** (line 10) _____

❏ 2. **refutation** (line 12) _____

❏ 3. **intention** (line 14) _____

❏ 4. **coherence** (line 17) _____

❏ 5. **diction** (line 18) _____

SET TWO

| the suggestive meaning of a word | the direct meaning of a word | the process of changing |
| the use of corresponding syntactical forms | a restatement of a passage using other words | |

❏ 6. **denotation** (line 19) _____

❏ 7. **connotation** (line 20) _____

❏ 8. **transition** (line 22) _____

❏ 9. **parallelism** (line 24) _____

❏ 10. **paraphrase** (line 27) _____

▮▮▮▮▮ SELF-TESTS

1 Circle the correct meaning of each vocabulary word.

1. connotation: direct meaning   suggestive meaning

2. diction: choice of words   choice of type size

3. parallelism: contrast in parts   similarity in aspects

4. paraphrase: to use an author's words to express in other words

5. refutation: disproving a statement   agreeing with a statement

6. transition: staying in the same place process of changing

7. coherence: illogical organization   orderly relationship

8. denotation: suggestive meaning   direct meaning

9. intention: a plan   clueless

10. thesis: a proposal   a refusal

2 Match a word to each example.

1. later, while, furthermore, finally _____

2. mother: a female parent _____

3. According to Austen it isn't how long it takes, but how good it is that matters. _____

4. I *really want* a new car. I *desire* a new car. I *need* a new car. _____

5. Over the weekend, the children read books, drew pictures, and made cupcakes.

   _____

6. mother: the person who made me cookies and tucked me into bed _____

7. Some people in the company believe the change in policy is causing problems, but they need to look ahead and see that after some initial scheduling problems, all employees will have more time to spend on leisure pursuits. For example, when the rotation begins . . . _____

8. The school needs to offer more math classes so that students can graduate on time.

   _____

9. The plan is to get up at 6:00 and be on the road by 6:30. _____

10. Outline: Summer can cause special problems for some people. _____
    I. A greater chance of getting sunburned
    II. Dehydration
    III. Heat exhaustion

3 Finish the sentences using the vocabulary words. Use each word once.

1. The sentence "On my vacation I will have time to hike, to relax, and visiting with friends" is confusing because it doesn't use _____.

2. The _____ of my research paper is that more Neighborhood Watch programs will make our city safer.

3. Because I was writing for children, I paid extra attention to my _____. I didn't want to use words they wouldn't understand.

4. I was confused when reading Isabel's paper because it lacked _____. First she told about a trip to a farm and then she described her math test, and her topic was supposed to be about a favorite building.

5. It can be hard to _____ because you want to get the writer's idea correct, but you can't use any of the writer's key words or the same sentence pattern.

6. When I mentioned the word *dog* in class, I found out that the _____ varied from a cute poodle to a mean Doberman depending on people's experiences.

7. The _____ of the orientation meeting was to help students understand the campus, not to confuse them.

8. I thought my idea for the party was the best, but after Tony _____ my points, I saw how expensive and impractical my plan was.

9. The dictionary helped me with the _____ for the word *love*, but I know that in most people's minds the word means more than "an intense affectionate concern for another person."

10. By using the _____ phrases *for instance* and *to illustrate*, I remember to put examples in my papers, which makes them more interesting to read.

WORD WISE

Context Clue Mini-Lesson 3

This lesson uses examples to explain the unknown word. The examples may consist of one illustration of the word or be a list of items. In the paragraph below, circle the examples you find that clarify the meaning of the underlined words. Then use the examples to write your own definitions on the lines next to the words that follow the paragraph.

Lucelia had always been a steadfast friend. She came to visit me daily when I was in the hospital, and she wrote to me weekly when I lived overseas for a year. She had also always been easy to talk to and quite vociferous in her opinions. She never hesitated to tell me what brand to buy or who to vote for. I was, therefore, shocked when she came over one night and refused to say anything. She just sat on my couch trembling. I tried to elicit a response by asking her questions like "Are you sick?" or "Do you want a cup of tea?" After an hour she opened up and told me that she had seen an apparition. She had seen her dead grandmother before and that hadn't seemed to bother her much. This time she said she had seen Napoleon, and seeing a famous person had really scared her.

Your Definition

1. Steadfast _____

2. Vociferous _____

3. Elicit _____

4. Apparition _____

Write a paragraph on your attitude toward writing. Use six examples of the vocabulary words in your paragraph. Label the words when you have finished the paragraph. For example, if you write, "After I am done writing, I am usually proud of the hard work I put into it," make an arrow to the transition word *After* and write *transition* in the margin.

_____

_____

_____

_____

_____

_____

_____

_____

_____

_____

_____

_____

_____

HINT

Test Taking Strategies

Of course, studying is essential to do well on a test, but for some people that isn't enough to ease the stress that testing can bring. A few strategies may help you deal with test anxiety. A healthy body leads to a good test taking experience, so get a good night's rest and eat a healthy breakfast, lunch, or dinner before the exam. Exercise before the exam. Take a walk or do some stretching to help you relax. When you get to the classroom, take a few deep breaths and visualize yourself in a soothing spot such as hiking in a forest or taking a bath. Also picture yourself as being successful at the test; don't focus on any negatives. Being a bit nervous can help during a test by keeping you alert, but too much stress can ruin even the most prepared student's chances of success. If text anxiety becomes a serious problem for you, contact your college's counseling center for advice.

WORD LIST

coherence
[kō hēr' əns, kō her'-]

n. consistency; the quality of a logical or orderly relationship of parts

connotation
[kon' ə tā' shən]

n. the suggestive or associative meaning of a word beyond its literal definition

denotation
[dē' nō tā' shən]

n. the explicit or direct meaning of a word

diction
[dik' shən]

n. 1. the choice and use of words in speech or writing
2. distinctness of speech

intention
[in ten' shən]

n. a plan; an aim that guides action

parallelism
[par' ə lel iz' əm]

n. 1. the use of corresponding syntactical forms
2. likeness or similarity in aspect

paraphrase
[par' ə frāz']

n. a restatement of a passage using other words
v. to express in a paraphrase

refutation
[ref' yoo tā' shən]

n. 1. the act of disproving a statement or argument
2. something that disproves

thesis
[thē' sis]

n. a proposal that is defended by argument

transition
[tran zish' ən]

n. the process of changing from one subject or activity to another

WORDS TO WATCH

Which words would you like to practice with a bit more? Pick 3–5 words to study and list them below. Write the word, its definition, and compose your own sentence using the word correctly. This extra practice could be the final touch to learning a word.

Word	Definition	Your Sentence
1. _____	_____	_____
2. _____	_____	_____
3. _____	_____	_____
4. _____	_____	_____
5. _____	_____	_____

9 Theater

Behind the Curtain

Our tour is in luck. Let's stop for a few minutes behind the curtain and listen as our two resident playwrights discuss ideas for this summer's new play.

5   **HENRIK:**   I've been thinking about the play we are writing, and I'd like the **antagonist** to be a woman named June. I find that it often surprises the audience when a woman is the adversary.

    LORRAINE: That's fine with me, Henrik, and I was thinking the **protagonist** should be a woman named Colleen.
10   There aren't enough female leads in the theater.

    HENRIK: Sure, having two major female roles will be great for costuming. The play is going to be performed in the large **amphitheater,** so we can use the women's strong personalities to design outfits with dramatic
15   colors that can be easily seen from all the seats. In fact, I think Colleen's **hubris** should be about her appearance. Her pride in her looks will be her major flaw and almost cause her downfall.

    LORRAINE: Great idea! I know we aren't writing a tragedy, but we do want some **pathos** in the play. The audience should feel sympathy or
20   pity for both leads. In the **prologue** let's start by telling the audience about the longtime feud between these two women.

    HENRIK: Good, we will set up the conflict before the play begins. Then June and Colleen should each have a **monologue** at some point in the play. They should each have a long solo speech to tell their
25   feelings and history.

    LORRAINE: Who should the **ingénue** be? I was thinking Colleen's sister Alicia would be the perfect innocent young woman. We won't, however, make her so sweet that she steals the **limelight** from the other characters.

30   **HENRIK:**   No, she shouldn't grab any scenes from the stars. We would still have Colleen speak the **epilogue** where she sums up the play and says something to get the audience applauding.

    LORRAINE: Yes, that's it. Now all we have to do is develop the conflict, decide on the climax, write the dialogue, and we've got ourselves a play.

For each set, write the definition on the line next to the word to which it belongs. If you are unsure, return to the reading on page 58, and underline any context clues you find. After you've made your predictions, check your answers against the Word List on page 63. Place a checkmark in the box next to each word whose definition you missed. These are the words you'll want to study closely.

SET ONE

an adversary	arrogance	the leading character
a feeling of sympathy	a round structure with seats rising from an open space in the center	

❑ 1. **antagonist** (line 5) _____

❑ 2. **protagonist** (line 9) _____

❑ 3. **amphitheater** (line 13) _____

❑ 4. **hubris** (line 16) _____

❑ 5. **pathos** (line 19) _____

SET TWO

an innocent young woman	a long solo speech	the lines introducing a play
a speech made after the end of a play	the focus of attention	

❑ 6. **prologue** (line 20) _____

❑ 7. **monologue** (line 23) _____

❑ 8. **ingénue** (line 26) _____

❑ 9. **limelight** (line 28) _____

❑ 10. **epilogue** (line 31) _____

SELF-TESTS

1 Put a T for true or F for false next to each statement.

_____ 1. An antagonist in a play might try to blackmail the hero.

_____ 2. An ingénue is likely to punch someone in the face.

_____ 3. If you arrive fifteen minutes late to a play, you have probably missed the epilogue.

_____ 4. You might want a seat cushion in an amphitheater.

_____ 5. During a scene with a sick child, most people would feel pathos.

_____ 6. The protagonist is usually in a play for only ten or fifteen minutes.

_____ 7. After an actor wins an Oscar, he is likely to be in the limelight for a while.

_____ 8. The prologue is usually given just before the first intermission.

_____ 9. A person's hubris can cause him or her to forget about other people's feelings.

_____ 10. Listening to a friend's monologue can be frustrating when you have something you want to say.

2 Finish the reading using the vocabulary words. Use each word once.

VOCABULARY LIST

protagonist	pathos	limelight	hubris	antagonist
prologue	monologue	ingénue	epilogue	amphitheater

FARM LIVING

When the curtain parts, the (1)_____, Diana, is standing in front of a garden with a smile on her sweet, young face. In the (2)_____ she tells the audience that the play is about how the family farm is going to be taken away from them.

Then an evil laugh is heard offstage, and the (3)_____, the cruel and rich Mr. Roth, enters. He opposes Diana's father, Rudolph, the (4)_____ in the play.

Whenever Rudolph bounds onto the stage, he steals the (5)_____. He is so forceful that he can't help but be the center of attention. During his (6)_____ the audience is hushed. Diana too has her moments. She arouses the audience's (7)_____ when she falls, sprains her ankle, and hobbles home to find a sign out front. There isn't a dry eye in the (8)_____, when she cries out, "It's been sold!" In the end, however, Mr. Roth's (9)_____ causes his downfall. He believes in cruelty, and he is shocked when the town rallies behind Diana and Rudolph to get the farm back. The (10)_____ adds the surprising but happy information that Mr. Roth changes his ways and marries Diana.

3 Complete the following analogies. See Completing Analogies on page 6 for instructions and practice.

1. Black Beauty : horse :: Little Miss Muffet : _____
2. kindness : cruelty :: _____ : friend
3. steering wheel : car :: seat : _____
4. windy day : flower pot falls over :: end of a play : _____
5. comedian : _____ :: chef : mixing bowl
6. a flat tire : a problem :: bride at a wedding : _____
7. forbid : prohibit :: _____ : arrogance
8. cat : pet :: Sherlock Holmes : _____
9. play begins : _____ :: unlock a door : walk in
10. a friend is robbed : _____ :: you win the lottery : happiness

WORD WISE

Collocations

The company is going through a *transition period* as we learn to incorporate more technology into our services. (Chapter 8)

The actor thought he would enjoy being *in the limelight,* but after a few months of photographers camped out in front of his house, he grew tired of it. (Chapter 9)

Word Pairs

Denotation/Connotation: Denotation (Chapter 8) means "the explicit or direct meaning of a word." Connotation (Chapter 8) means "the suggestive or associative meaning of a word beyond its literal definition." The denotation of *work* is "employment to earn one's living." The connotation of *work* for many people suggests a place filled with squabbles and unreasonable demands.

Antagonist/Protagonist: Antagonist (Chapter 9) means "one who opposes and competes with someone else." Protagonist (Chapter 9) means "any leading figure." The protagonist in a work of fiction has to face an antagonist at some point to create the excitement conflict causes.

Where Did It Come From?

Limelight (Chapter 9): had its start in the theater world. It comes from quicklime, a popular term for calcium oxide which gives off a brilliant white light when heated. It was originally called a "Drummond light," after its inventor Thomas Drummond (1797–1840), but came to be known as a "limelight." The limelight was used as a spotlight in English theaters. Other forms of lights are now used in theaters, but a person in "a position as the focus of attention" is still referred to as being in the limelight.

Pretend that the play discussed in the reading on page 58 has been finished and performed. You are a reviewer for the local newspaper and have just been to opening night. Write a review of the play that includes a recommendation as to whether or not your readers should see the play. Use at least seven of the vocabulary words in your review.

_____

_____

_____

_____

_____

_____

_____

_____

_____

_____

_____

_____

_____

HINT

Make Your Own Tests

A great way to study is to make your own tests in the same style of the tests that you will have in class. Making the tests puts you in the instructor's frame of mind and makes you think about what is important to study.

- Before the first test (or quiz), ask your instructor what format(s) the test will be in— true/false, multiple choice, matching, essay.
- Create a test in the same format(s) with questions that you think will be asked, neatly handwritten or typed.
- Set the test aside for a day.
- The next day, take the test and correct yourself. How much did you remember?
- Make a test for a friend and exchange with each other. Did you come up with similar questions?
- If you examine the first in-class test, you will have a better idea of what the instructor is looking for, and then your homemade tests will be even more useful.

▰▰▰ WORD LIST

amphitheater
[am' fə thē' ə tər]

n. an oval or round structure with tiers of seats rising from an open space in the center used for plays or contests

antagonist
[an tag' ə nist]

n. one who opposes and competes with someone else; an adversary

epilogue
[ep' ə lôg', -log']

n. 1. a short poem or speech made to the audience after the end of a play
2. a brief addition at the end of a literary work, often telling the characters' futures

hubris
[hyoo' bris]

n. arrogance; extreme pride

ingénue
[an' zhe noo']

n. 1. an innocent young woman
2. an actress playing an ingénue

limelight
[līm' līt']

n. a position as the focus of attention

monologue
[mon' ə lôg', -log']

n. a long solo speech

pathos
[pā' thos, -thōs]

n. a feeling of sympathy or pity

prologue
[prō' lôg, -log]

n. 1. the lines introducing a play
2. an introductory event

protagonist
[prō tag' ə nist]

n. 1. the leading character in a work of literature
2. any leading figure

▰▰▰ WORDS TO WATCH

Which words would you like to practice with a bit more? Pick 3–5 words to study and list them below. Write the word, its definition, and compose your own sentence using the word correctly. This extra practice could be the final touch to learning a word.

	Word	Definition	Your Sentence
1.			
2.			
3.			
4.			
5.			

10 Review

Focus on Chapters 1–9

The following activities give you a chance to interact some more with the vocabulary words you've been learning. By looking at art, taking tests, answering questions, doing a crossword puzzle, and working with others, you will see which words you know well and which you still need to work with.

1. _____

2. _____

3. _____

4. _____

5. _____

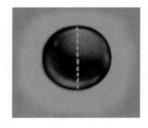

6. _____

7. _____

8. _____

9. _____

10. _____

11. _____

12. _____

■■■■■ ART

Match each picture on page 64 to one of the following vocabulary words. Use each word once.

VOCABULARY LIST

connoisseur	stratification	hail	connotation	cacophony	bisect
ostracize	placate	taboo	symmetrical	emoticon	destitute

■■■■■ SELF-TESTS

1A Pick the word that best completes each sentence.

1. My sister said she needed her _____, so she moved out of our apartment.

   a. fallacy   b. cacophony   c. autonomy   d. cinematography

2. I will do my _____ to make sure you enjoy your vacation while you are staying with me.

   a. taboo   b. utmost   c. jargon   d. decorum

3. Since its _____ there have been only disagreements on how to operate the policy.

   a. inception   b. interval   c. montage   d. martyrdom

4. The _____ in the auditorium could be improved: I thought the president of the college said, "Welcome to the graduation cemetery."

   a. genre   b. acoustics   c. encryption   d. ambivalence

5. Some _____ experiences differ among cultures, such as initiation ceremonies into adulthood.

   a. trace   b. enigma   c. repertoire   d. socialization

6. I thought it was a _____ that people need eight hours of sleep each night, but when I fell asleep in my soup, I realized I couldn't get by on two hours of sleep for long.

   a. fallacy   b. variable   c. hubris   d. paraphrase

7. The character's _____ was moving; she really explained how sad her childhood had been.

   a. gradation   b. clamor   c. monologue   d. netiquette

1B Complete the following sentences using the vocabulary words. Use each word once.

a. modulate	b. denotation	c. juxtaposition	d. prologue	e. encryption

1. _____ has become essential to communication today; I don't think people would use the Internet so much unless they were assured of some privacy.

2. The _____ of the painting of the starving man next to the one of the king in his finery helped show why the French were upset with the aristocracy.

3. The speaker had to _____ his voice as the air conditioning went on and off.

4. The _____ of the play told too much; there was no suspense when the murderer was revealed.

5. The _____ of *work* certainly doesn't cover all the gossiping and fighting I see in my office every day.

2 Finish the story using the vocabulary words. Use each word once.

VOCABULARY LIST

alleviate	audible	deviate	interval	status
ambivalence	cacophony	disconcerted	limelight	surreal
attune	clamor	enigma	magnitude	transition

NOT MEANT TO BE

The situation at my house was (1)_____. Every time I sat down to study, someone started making noise. When my sister turned on the television, I asked her to turn it down, but it was still (2)_____ in my room. After she left, my neighbor started a(n) (3)_____. Bob decided it was the perfect time to build the shed he had been talking about for ten years! He was sawing and pounding for over an hour. My (4)_____ as a top student was quickly falling as the noises around me continued. The (5)_____ grew worse when my mother turned on the mixer to make

a cake, and my dad turned the radio up to listen to his favorite song. How I was going to study with so much noise around me was a(n) (6)_____ to me. I quickly became (7)_____ as I saw the Student-of the-Year Award slip out of my grasp. The (8)_____ of my problems finally hit me: I could fail if I didn't do something right away. I was going to have to (9)_____ from my original plan.

During a brief (10)_____ when Bob ran inside to answer his phone and my dad turned down his music, I had time to think. There was only one way to (11)_____ the noise problem. With some (12)_____, I turned from my faithful desk where I had spent many happy hours studying and left my room. I was going to have to go to the library and

(13) _____ myself to a new environment. The (14) _____ wouldn't be easy, but I was willing to try. I couldn't dream of giving up the (15) _____ I enjoyed in my role as an excellent student. I would adapt to my new circumstances.

▮▮▮▮ INTERACTIVE EXERCISE

Answer the following questions to further test your understanding of the vocabulary words.

1. What is your favorite genre to read? _____

2. What are two restaurant chains that are ubiquitous in your area?

   _____   _____

3. Name a field that uses a lot of statistics.

   _____

4. Name two norms for classroom behavior.

   _____   _____

5. What is one step we can take to stop persecution in society?

   _____

   _____

6. Name two newsgroups you would be interested in joining.

   _____   _____

7. If decorum were required at a party, describe two ways a person would act.

   _____

   _____

8. Besides looks, in what two other areas might people display their hubris?

   _____

   _____

9. Give two examples of jargon from the medical, legal, or computer fields.

   _____

   _____

10. Name two Olympic sports in which the execution of the activity is scored.

    _____   _____

11. What are two ways people can improve their diction?

    _____

    _____

12. Give the name of the antagonist in a book you have read or a movie you have seen.

    _____

CROSSWORD PUZZLE

Use the following words to complete the crossword puzzle. You will use each word once.

VOCABULARY LIST

amphitheater	ascertain	censure
cinematography	coherence	conventional
epilogue	epitomize	finite
flame	gradation	induce
ingénue	intention	martyrdom
montage	neophyte	netiquette
parallelism	paraphrase	pathos
pervasive	protagonist	prototype
quota	refutation	repertoire
thesis	transgression	variable

Across
3. consistency
7. violation of a law or duty
8. spreading throughout
11. a pattern
13. a feeling of sympathy
14. an allotment
15. works an artist can present
17. having bounds or limits
21. an addition at the end of a literary work
24. a restatement of a passage
25. a leading figure, ex. Indiana Jones
27. to rant
28. online manners
29. the art of motion-picture photography
30. a plan

Down
1. extreme suffering
2. an official reprimand
4. customary
5. a proposal defended by argument
6. a structure used for plays
9. changeable
10. to learn with certainty
12. likeness in aspect
16. a beginner
18. innocent young woman
19. the act of disproving a statement
20. a stage in a series
22. to typify
23. a film editing technique
26. to persuade

HINT

Shades of Meaning

Learning new vocabulary is more than learning synonyms. While some words you learn may be similar to other words you know and may be used in place of another word, every word is unique. Good writers choose their words carefully. Words have different shades of meaning, and conscientious writers think about those differences when picking a word to use. A careful reader also responds to those differences in meaning. In some cases the differences are slight, such as "On Sundays I eat a big dinner" or "On Sundays I eat a large dinner." But replacing "big" or "large" with "huge" or "gigantic" (both synonyms for "big") does alter the image of how much food the person is eating. Some synonyms have even bigger differences. For the sentence, "The clever woman found a way to get out of debt," "clever" could be replaced with the synonyms "smart" or "crafty." The reader would have a different reaction to the woman depending on whether the writer selected "smart" or "crafty." When reading or writing, pay attention to the diverse ways words can be used.

MIX IT UP

MATCHING MEANINGS

Get six to eight classmates together, and make teams of three to four people. You will need two sets of flash cards. Lay out a square of 25 flash cards with the words face up. Lay out another square of the same 25 words with the definitions face up. One person on a team picks up a word and tries to find the matching definition in the other square. Teammates can help the person. If the person is right, he or she gets to keep both cards. If the person is wrong, he or she returns the cards to their places. A team can keep going until they miss a match. When all the words and definitions are matched, the team with the most cards wins. This activity can also be played with pairs, or you can test yourself individually if you have two sets of flash cards (or you can write the words on slips of paper and match them to the definition side of your flash cards).

Planning for the Future

$FINANCIAL INSIGHTS

FALL 2006

INVESTMENT REALITIES

When investing in the stock market, keeping a few points in mind will help you feel more confident about the experience.

5   Don't expect to triple your investment in a few months. **Affluence** doesn't just happen; it takes careful planning. For most people, letting one's investments grow over time is the way to get rich.

10   Remain **resolute** even when the market falters. A **volatile** market can scare people, but changes in the market, even explosive ones, are usual—remain firm. Don't buy and sell without a plan.

15   Look carefully at the fees **levied** by a broker. Do you pay when you buy or when you sell? Are there monthly or yearly fees? What kinds of transaction fees are imposed?

20   No one person has a **monopoly** on sound investing. Read the newspaper and business journals to keep up on your investments. Check out books on the stock market or attend a seminar to learn
25   more about how your money can work for you. You may also want to find a **confidant** to discuss business matters with: having a person you can share private information with can make you
30   feel more secure about your decisions.

MAKE TIME TO MEET

It is a wise person who sets aside time for a **biannual** meeting with a financial advisor to discuss one's **portfolio**. Every six months call your financial planner and 35 ask him or her to meet with you to discuss your holdings.

The following are some questions you will want to consider:

How are my stocks and other investments 40 doing? Should I further diversify? What kinds of **fluctuations** have there been in the stock market? If there have been changes in the market, how should I change my investing patterns? How much 45 **equity** do I have in my house? What should I do with that money? How close am I to retirement, and how does that change my investing strategy?

||||||| PREDICTING

For each set, write the definition on the line next to the word to which it belongs. If you are unsure, return to the reading on page 70, and underline any context clues you find. After you've made your predictions, check your answers against the Word List on page 75. Place a checkmark in the box next to each word whose definition you missed. These are the words you'll want to study closely.

SET ONE

| wealth | unstable | imposed or collected | showing firmness | exclusive control |

☐ 1. **affluence** (line 6) _____

☐ 2. **resolute** (line 10) _____

☐ 3. **volatile** (line 11) _____

☐ 4. **levied** (line 15) _____

☐ 5. **monopoly** (line 20) _____

SET TWO

| happening twice each year | irregular variations | the value of a business or property |
| a list of investments | | a person one can share private matters with |

☐ 6. **confidant** (line 27) _____

☐ 7. **biannual** (line 33) _____

☐ 8. **portfolio** (line 34) _____

☐ 9. **fluctuations** (line 42) _____

☐ 10. **equity** (line 46) _____

||||||| SELF-TESTS

1 In each group, circle the word that does not have a connection to the other three words.

EXAMPLE: case   folder   (cabinet)   portfolio

A case, folder, and portfolio are all portable items one could use to carry papers, but a cabinet is too heavy to carry.

1. confidant	close	public	private
2. exclusive	one	shared	monopoly
3. firmness	unchanging	weakness	resolute
4. poor	rich	affluence	abundance
5. semiannual	weekly	twice	biannual
6. impose	levy	collect	give

7.	volatile	fleeting	constant	changeable
8.	justness	equity	fairness	unequal
9.	variation	sameness	fluctuation	change
10.	debts	portfolio	holdings	investments

2 Finish the headlines from fictitious newspapers. Use each word once.

VOCABULARY LIST

confidant	resolute	portfolio	volatile	fluctuation
biannual	equity	monopoly	levy	affluence

1. **Despite Pouring Rain, Protestors Remain _____ :
   They Won't Go Home**

2. **Grocery Wants to _____ Fee for Use of Shopping Carts**

3. *Study Reports _____ of Most Americans Twice as High
   as Fifty Years Ago*

4. **_____ Discovered in Germany Could Contain
   Drawings by DaVinci**

5. **County _____ Sale of Overstocked Supplies Offers
   Deals for Citizens**

6. **Wild _____ of Winter Temperatures Spells Disaster for Farmers**

7. *Part-time Workers Nationwide Look for _____ in
   Health Benefits*

8. Hi-Tech Corporation Charged with Unfair _____ of
   New Software

9. ***Diplomat's _____ Revealed as Foreign Spy***

10. **_____ Political Situation in North Africa Keeps Area
    Unsafe for Tourists**

3 Finish the reading. Use each word once.

CHANGING NEEDS

After my recent (1)_____ meeting with my financial advisor, I am ready to make some new investments. The review of my (2)_____ shows that I am in fair financial shape, but I could be more aggressive. I have been (3)_____ and kept my stocks when the market plunged. However, some of the market (4)_____ have made it a good idea to change a few of my investments. Although it looks like the (5)_____ period is over, I want to explore my options.

   Then my neighbor told me about a company that has invented a machine that can suck up the dust in a house in two minutes. They have a(n) (6)_____ on building the machine. If I invest ten thousand dollars now, I will be assured (7)_____ for life. I wonder if I should use the (8)_____ in my house to get a loan. My neighbor has to (9)_____ a four-hundred-dollar fee for providing me with this tip, but I'll make that back and so much more when the Sucker goes on the market. I said I'd have to discuss this opportunity with my (10)_____ before making a decision. What do you think?

WORD WISE

Context Clue Mini-Lesson 4

This lesson uses the general meaning of a sentence or passage to help you understand the meaning of the underlined word. In the paragraph below, circle any words that give you clues to the meaning. Write your definitions of the underlined words in the blanks that follow the paragraph.

   The area looked devoid of any chance for life. The ground was hard and the few plants around looked dead. But the pioneers felt the land was arable. They carefully tended the land, and within five years it was transformed into a verdant paradise. Orchards of apples and pears sprinkled the landscape; lettuce, corn, and other vegetables filled the fields; and flowering trees adorned each yard. The pioneers had known that to cultivate the area all they needed was patience and hard work, which they had gladly supplied.

Your Definition

1. Devoid _____

2. Arable _____

3. Verdant _____

4. Cultivate _____

▐▌▌▌▌ INTERACTIVE EXERCISE

Write short responses for each of the following items.

1. List someone you consider a confidant. _____

2. Tell about a time when you were resolute. _____
_____

3. Name three people who symbolize affluence.
_____ _____ _____

4. Describe a fluctuation you have experienced. _____
_____

5. List two kinds of equity for which workers fight.
_____ _____

6. List three situations that could easily become volatile.
_____
_____
_____

7. List two places where a fee might be levied.
_____ _____

8. Name two professions where someone would likely carry a portfolio.
_____ _____

9. State two activities that people should do at least biannually.
_____ _____

10. Name two items the government has a monopoly on.

_____ _____

HINT

Easy Questions First

If you get stuck on one question when doing a multiple-choice or matching test go on to the next one. When you finish answering the questions that are easy for you, see which questions and choices are left. With fewer choices, the answers should be easier to find. For an example of where you can use this technique look back at Self-Test 2 in this chapter.

WORD LIST

affluence
[af′ l⨪o̅o̅ əns]
n. 1. wealth; an abundance
2. a flowing toward

biannual
[bī an′ y⨪o̅o̅ əl]
adj. happening twice each year; semiannual

confidant
[kon′ fi dant′, -dänt′, kon′ fi dant′, -dänt′]
n. a person one can share private matters and problems with; a close friend

equity
[ek′ wə tē]
n. 1. the value of a business or property (a house) beyond any mortgage or liability
2. the quality of being fair

fluctuation
[fluk′ ch⨪o̅o̅ a′ shən]
n. an irregular variation; the result of such a variation

levy
[lev′ ē]
v. to impose or to collect, such as a tax

monopoly
[mə nop′ ə lē]
n. 1. exclusive control over anything
2. exclusive control by one group of the means of producing or selling a product or service

portfolio
[pôrt fō′ lē ō′]
n. 1. a list of the investments owned by a bank, investment organization, or other investor
2. a portable case for holding loose sheets of paper or drawings

resolute
[rez′ ə l⨪o̅o̅t′]
adj. showing firmness; unwavering

volatile
[vol′ ə til]
adj. 1. unstable; changeable
2. threatening to break out into violence; explosive
3. evaporating rapidly

WORDS TO WATCH

Which words would you like to practice with a bit more? Pick 3–5 words to study and list them below. Write the word, its definition, and compose your own sentence using the word correctly. This extra practice could be the final touch to learning a word.

	Word	Definition	Your Sentence
1.			
2.			
3.			
4.			
5.			

CHAPTER 12

World History

The Temples of Angkor

In the jungles of Cambodia sit a **multitude** of temples built during the reign of the Khmer Empire between the ninth and fifteenth centuries. Each **successive** king built his own **enclave** consisting of
5 religious temples, administrative buildings, and royal palaces. Each king felt that to **procure** his place in history he had to build his own temple complex, and about fifty sites have been discovered in the Angkor region. (Angkor means "city" or "capital.") Only
10 religious buildings could be made of stone, and they are the only structures that have survived.

The kings were highly **venerated** and may have been worshipped as gods. Many of the temple statues feature the god favored by the ruling king and often the king himself as a god. The **depictions** of the rulers were usually linked to either Hinduism or Buddhism. Surayavarman II, who began his rule in 1112, started the construction of the largest and most magnificent of the complexes: Angkor
15 Wat. It was begun in the early part of his reign and was not completed until after his death in 1152. He was a devotee of the Hindu god Vishnu and incorporated several statues of Vishnu into the complex to assert his rule and beliefs. A few decades later, the powerful king Jayavarman VII, who ruled from 1181–1219, began a building spree. He built Ta Prahm to honor his parents and Preah Khan and the Bayon, which features hundreds of carved faces of himself as a Buddhist god. Jayavarman was also
20 responsible for building more roads and reservoirs and expanding the kingdom into present day Thailand, southern Laos, and southern Vietnam.

The statues and temples at Angkor are **potent** symbols of the power of the kings, and they provide most of the historical records of the period as little writing was done or kept. The beautifully decorated carvings on the temples depict events of religious significance, of a king's achievements, and of everyday
25 life. Among the stories on the walls are scenes of battles between the Khmer and the Cham people of current day Vietnam and encounters with warriors from the kingdoms that are now part of Thailand. The area also became a trading center and goods such as cloth, rice, slaves, and buffalo were
30 exchanged. At various times over ten thousand people lived at Angkor, including, according to an inscription on one temple complex, "615 dancing girls." For most of the Khmer people many hours were spent working in the fields and completing the
35 numerous building projects. Although periods of war were significant events in their lives, times of celebration were also important during these years.

The empire began to **wane** in the fourteenth century, and an invasion from Thailand in 1431 led
40 to the destruction of much of the Angkor way of life. The Khmer gradually left the area, never to return. The **profuse** jungle growth reclaimed much of the land and hid the monuments for four hundred years, waiting for **posterity** to discover them again.

PREDICTING

For each set, write the definition on the line next to the word to which it belongs. If you are unsure, return to the reading on page 76, and underline any context clues you find. After you've made your predictions, check your answers against the Word List on page 81. Place a checkmark in the box next to each word whose definition you missed. These are the words you'll want to study closely.

SET ONE

| a bounded area enclosed within a larger area | regarded with respect | the quality of being numerous |
| consecutive | to obtain | |

☐ 1. **multitude** (line 1) _____

☐ 2. **successive** (line 4) _____

☐ 3. **enclave** (line 4) _____

☐ 4. **procure** (line 6) _____

☐ 5. **venerated** (line 11) _____

SET TWO

| powerful | plentiful | to decrease | future generations |
| representations in a picture or sculpture | | | |

☐ 6. **depictions** (line 12) _____

☐ 7. **potent** (line 22) _____

☐ 8. **wane** (line 38) _____

☐ 9. **profuse** (line 41) _____

☐ 10. **posterity** (line 42) _____

SELF-TESTS

1 Match each word with its synonym in Set One and its antonym in Set Two.

SYNONYMS

SET ONE

_____ 1. depiction   a. consecutive

_____ 2. profuse   b. future

_____ 3. enclave   c. enclosure

_____ 4. successive   d. abundant

_____ 5. posterity   e. portrayal

ANTONYMS

_____ 6. procure   f. increase

_____ 7. multitude   g. give

_____ 8. venerate   h. degrade

_____ 9. potent   i. few

_____ 10. wane   j. useless

2 Pick the best word to complete each sentence. Use each word once.

VOCABULARY LIST

profuse	waned	multitude	successive	enclave
potent	depicted	procure	venerate	posterity

1. My enthusiasm for the project _____ as people began to argue with each other at every meeting.

2. My brother was able to _____ two seats to the sold-out concert for us through his business connections.

3. I had to hand my paper in late because of a(n) _____ of problems, from being sick to computer failures.

4. My doctor gave me some _____ medicine; I was better in one day.

5. We should _____ our nation's teachers because they have much of the responsibility for educating the future.

6. Her thank-yous were _____, but I didn't feel I deserved that much gratitude.

7. We are vacationing at the Erikson family _____ in the Rocky Mountains. My great-grandfather constructed the cabins and other buildings in the 1800s.

8. I didn't like the way my friend _____ me in his short story. Why was I the villain?

9. Each _____ generation has to deal with some of the problems created by the generations who came before.

10. It would be nice if _____ would remember us as a peace-loving people, but the number of wars in the twentieth century probably makes that hope unrealistic.

3 Answer each question with the appropriate vocabulary word. Use each word once.

VOCABULARY LIST

profuse	waned	venerate	successive	enclave
potent	depiction	procure	posterity	multitude

1. Matt has to feed 300 people. What term would describe this group? _____

2. Alexander needs to get food and drinks for the party. What does he need to do?

_____

3. Colleen thinks her Grandpa is the smartest man in the world. How does she feel about him? _____

4. You can smell a woman's perfume four aisles from you in the movie theater. What word would you use to describe it? _____

5. Most people today want to keep the air and oceans clean. Who are they saving them for? _____

6. We can no longer see our neighbor's front door because the ivy has grown over it. How would you describe the growth in the neighbor's yard? _____

7. You see a sculpture of Benjamin Franklin signing *The Declaration of Independence*. What would you call the sculpture? _____

8. After two years of studying biology, it no longer excites Marin. What has happened to her interest in the subject? _____

9. Within an hour, Anders stubbed his toe getting out of bed, spilled coffee on himself, and got a flat tire on the way to school. What would you call the problems that happened to him? _____

10. At the zoo there is an enclosed area for the primates with an island, a jungle area, and a hospital for newborns. What would this area be called? _____

WORD WISE

Collocations

The state has decided to *levy a fee* for using all its parks whether people come for an afternoon picnic or to camp overnight. (Chapter 11)

By keeping Frieda and Jorge apart, we avoided a *volatile situation;* they still blame each other for losing the big account. (Chapter 11)

The town's new statue dedicated to endangered animals is a *potent reminder* of how we all need to work to protect the environment. (Chapter 12)

In some cultures grandparents are *highly venerated* for their years of accumulated wisdom. (Chapter 12)

Word Pairs

Volatile/Stable: Volatile (Chapter 11) means "unstable, changeable." Stable means "constant; firm." When the government was taken over by the military, the economy was volatile with prices on items changing daily. When the president was put back in power, the country's economy returned to a stable state, and people knew a loaf of bread would be the same price for months.

Wax/Wane: Wax means "to increase" and wane (Chapter 12) means "to decrease." The moon waxes each month before the full moon and wanes after it.

Where Did It Come From?

Affluent (Chapter 11): comes from the Latin *ad* "to" plus *fluere* "flow" and meant "flowing abundantly." The plentiful flowing eventually came to mean "wealth or abundance."

Enclave (Chapter 12): comes from the Latin *en-* "in" and *clavis* "key" and meant an area that was "locked in." An enclave therefore is "any distinctly bounded area enclosed within a larger area." The country of Lesotho is an enclave of South Africa.

Finish the following who, what, where, when, and why lists to practice using the vocabulary words. Give two examples for each question.

1. Where would you find a multitude of people?

   _____   _____

2. Where would you find an enclave of buildings?

   _____   _____

3. What would you procure for a picnic?

   _____   _____

4. What are some potent smells?

   _____   _____

5. Whom do you venerate?

   _____   _____

6. Who do you think should be depicted on a coin?

   _____   _____

7. Why might a student's attention in class begin to wane?

   _____   _____

8. Why should we care about posterity?

   _____   _____

9. When would you want to make a profuse apology?

   _____   _____

10. When do you need to do something in successive steps?

   _____   _____

HINT

Finding a Time to Study

To make your study time effective, you need to find the time of day that you are most productive. Ask yourself whether you are a morning, afternoon, or night person. Don't try to get up early and study if you won't really be awake at that time. Or don't stay up late trying to read if all you want to do is close your eyes. Come to understand how your body works by paying attention to the times of the day when you feel the most tired and the most alert. Your study routine will be improved if you pay attention to your body clock.

▮▮▮ WORD LIST

depiction
[di pik' shən]

n. 1. a representation in a picture or sculpture
2. a representation in words; a description

enclave
[en' klāv, än'-]

n. 1. any distinctly bounded area enclosed within a larger area
2. a country or part of a country lying wholly within the boundaries of another

multitude
[mul' tə to͞od']

n. 1. the quality of being numerous
2. a great, indefinite number
3. the masses

posterity
[po ster' ə tē]

n. 1. future generations
2. all of a person's descendants

potent
[pōt' nt]

adj. 1. powerful
2. having great control or authority

procure
[prō kyoor', prə-]

v. 1. to obtain
2. to bring about

profuse
[prə fyo͞os', prō-]

adj. 1. plentiful; overflowing
2. extravagant

successive
[sək ses' iv]

adj. following in order; consecutive

venerate
[ven' ə rāt']

v. to regard with respect and reverence

wane
[wān]

v. 1. to decrease; to decline
2. to approach an end
n. a gradual declining

▮▮▮ WORDS TO WATCH

Which words would you like to practice with a bit more? Pick 3–5 words to study and list them below. Write the word, its definition, and compose your own sentence using the word correctly. This extra practice could be the final touch to learning a word.

	Word	Definition	Your Sentence
1.			
2.			
3.			
4.			
5.			

13 Geography

The Frozen Continent

Antarctica is a continent that has fascinated people for centuries. The **terrain** includes tall mountains (the highest is the Vinson Massif at 16,864 feet or 5,140 meters), active volcanoes, and valleys of rock that are surprisingly clear of any ice or snow. It

5 also contains the largest mass of ice in the world. The continent and the surrounding oceans contain more than 90% of the world's ice and 75% of its fresh water. Considering the cold temperatures of the continent, the abundance of ice is understandable. The record low for Antarctica is –128.5° F (–89.2° C) at Vostock

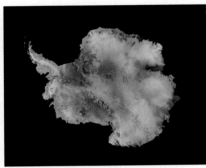

Antarctica—the peninsula juts out on the left side.

10 Station on the polar **plateau.** The average temperature at the South Pole is –59.8° F (–51° C). The Antarctica **Peninsula** is considerably warmer than the interior. During the winter, temperatures average 4° F (–20° C), and in the summer, temperatures get just above freezing or around 35–40° F (2–4° C). Despite the ice, Antarctica is one of the driest places on Earth. The interior of the continent is considered a polar

15 desert because it gets no rain and little snow. The peninsula gets more snow and some rain in the summer.

The cold makes the continent home to **nomads.** For the last two hundred years whalers, explorers, and scientists have made Antarctica home for short periods of time. Whalers were active in the Antarctic from the early 1900s to the 1960s. Serious scientific exploration of Antarctica began in the

20 1800s. Extreme **fortitude** was needed to be an explorer in the early days as clothing was not always as warm as was needed and transportation was difficult. Dogs and ponies were used to pull sleds, and at times the men were forced to pull their heavily laden sleds themselves. Among the **escapades** of the early explorers was a race to be the first to reach the South Pole. In 1911, Roald Amundsen of Norway and Robert Scott of Britain each undertook to reach the pole. Amundsen was the first to

25 arrive on December 14, 1911. Scott and his party arrived 33 days later to find the Norwegian flag and a tent left by Amundsen. Scott's journey had been filled with problems, which worsened on the return. One of the members of the **expedition,** Titus Oates, was suffering from frost-bitten feet. Oates feared he was slowing the team down, so one night during a blizzard he told the other men, "I am just going outside and may be some time." His **magnanimous** gesture was in vain. Strong storms continued, and

30 in a few days the rest of the group perished within eleven miles of the next supply station.

In the late 1950s, scientists saw the need to protect the **pristine** environment of Antarctica. Several nations (including Chile, Argentina, the United States, the Soviet Union, and Britain) cooperated to create the Antarctic Treaty. Every nation

35 that signs the treaty agrees to protect the plants and animals of the area, to refrain from mining, and to consider the environmental impact of any actions in the area. The treaty has been revised several times. Today the population of Antarctica **burgeons** in the summer with several countries reopening their research stations

40 after the harsh winter. Among the goals of these stations are to learn more about the plants and animals of this last great frontier and to preserve the unspoiled continent.

PREDICTING

For each set, write the definition on the line next to the word to which it belongs. If you are unsure, return to the reading on page 82, and underline any context clues you find. After you've made your predictions, check your answers against the Word List on page 87. Place a checkmark in the box next to each word whose definition you missed. These are the words you'll want to study closely.

SET ONE

| mental and emotional strength | a tract of land | an area of land almost fully surrounded by water |

a land area having a level surface considerably raised above adjoining land   wanderers

❏ 1. **terrain** (line 2) _____

❏ 2. **plateau** (line 10) _____

❏ 3. **peninsula** (line 11) _____

❏ 4. **nomads** (line 17) _____

❏ 5. **fortitude** (line 20) _____

SET TWO

adventures   unspoiled   a journey   grows   unselfish

❏ 6. **escapades** (line 22) _____

❏ 7. **expedition** (line 27) _____

❏ 8. **magnanimous** (line 29) _____

❏ 9. **pristine** (line 32) _____

❏ 10. **burgeons** (line 38) _____

SELF-TESTS

1 Put a T for true or F for false next to each statement.

_____ 1. Someone who has lived in the same house for 40 years would be considered a nomad.

_____ 2. Giving a fellow student a ride home after his car breaks down even though it is fifteen miles out of your way would be a magnanimous gesture.

_____ 3. A person needs fortitude to run a marathon.

_____ 4. One could swim all the way around a peninsula.

_____ 5. An expedition into the depths of a cave requires special gear.

_____ 6. A terrain filled with boulders would be easy to ride a bike on.

_____ 7. The city dump could be considered a pristine area.

_____ 8. Driving across the United States with only $80 in your pocket and no credit cards or other source of money could be considered an escapade.

_____ 9. A plant left in a dark room will likely burgeon.

_____ 10. Mount Everest would be considered a plateau.

2 Finish the journal entries using the vocabulary words. Use each word once.

SET ONE

VOCABULARY LIST

nomad   pristine   terrain   fortitude   expedition

January 16, 1914

We are preparing to leave the area. I am going to miss it here. Though the (1)_____ is covered with snow and the temperatures have been below freezing, it is a beautiful place. The (2)_____ nature of Antarctica attracts me. Everything is so pure and untouched by humans. The (3)_____ has been a success. We have done much research and made some fascinating discoveries. My (4)_____ has been tested by the whole journey, and I am proud to say that I have had the power to withstand the hardships. I do not think I will become a(n) (5)_____ wandering the Earth in search of adventure, but I have proved to myself that I can survive and appreciate the wilds of nature.

SET TWO

VOCABULARY LIST

magnanimous   escapade   plateau   peninsula   burgeoned

November 20, 1921

We have made it to the (6)_____, and it is a pleasure to see water again. The interior was much harsher than this area, and the climb up the (7)_____ exhausted me, especially since I had to take turns pulling our gear in the sled. Ernest has been quite (8)_____ and taken much longer pulls than I have. Tonight we rested and enjoyed watching the penguins. I thought I would be cursing myself for attempting this (9)_____, but I have done quite well. My confidence has (10)_____ as I have successfully dealt with each difficulty we have met on this expedition.

3 Match each example to the vocabulary word it best fits. Use each word once.

1. company earnings unchanged for three years _____
2. preparing oneself to speak in front of a crowd _____
3. an unexplored ice cave _____
4. a trek into the Amazon jungle _____
5. Marco Polo _____
6. the Kenai in Alaska, Yucatan in Mexico, or Jutland in Denmark _____
7. going to the doughnut shop during a blizzard _____
8. filled with boulders _____
9. wildflowers in the desert after a rainy season _____
10. letting someone else have the last cookie _____

WORD WISE

Internet Activity: Writing a Book Review

A perfect place to practice your newly acquired vocabulary is on the Internet. You can share your thoughts with others and use new words by writing a book review at amazon.com. This online bookstore has a space for you to write reviews of the books it sells. Go to their site and type in the name of a book you would like to review. You can pick a book you enjoyed reading or one that you disliked. It can be a work of fiction or nonfiction. You may even want to rate one of your textbooks. If Amazon sells the book, it will come up in a list of books. Go to the page for the book you want and click on the "Write a review" link. You will need to supply an e-mail address and a password before you can begin your review. Click on the "review guidelines" to read Amazon's rules for writing a review. Your review can be from 75 to 300 words. You will be asked to rate the book from 1 to 5 stars, supply a title for your review, and then write the review. Remember to use some of the vocabulary words you are learning in your review. You can use your real name on the review or create a pen name. Read through the directions for both to decide which you want to do. Most reviews are posted within one day. Once your review is posted, let your classmates know what book you reviewed. You can then read each others' reviews and practice reading the vocabulary words in new contexts. Your instructor may ask you to print out your review to display it in class or to read it aloud. Have fun sharing your opinions with the world and getting a chance to use your new knowledge in a real-life setting.

Pretend you are going on an expedition. Pick a place to travel to, consider going to someplace extremely cold or hot to test your fortitude, and write a journal entry describing your adventure. Use at least seven of the vocabulary words in your entry.

_____

_____

_____

_____

_____

_____

_____

_____

_____

_____

_____

_____

_____

_____

HINT

Creating Study Groups

A class can be more rewarding if you find classmates to study with. To create effective study groups, keep these points in mind.

- Get people who really want to learn, not just socialize.
- Pick a time that can accommodate most people; it may be impossible to get everyone together all the time. Exchange e-mail addresses and phone numbers so you can get a hold of each other to announce meeting times.
- Decide how often you will meet—twice a week, once a week, once a month.
- Pick a place to meet that promotes studying. See whether the library has study group rooms. You want a place where you can talk freely and where you won't be interrupted by the telephone, children, or other distractions.

WORD LIST

burgeon
[bûr′ jən]
v. to flourish; to grow; to sprout

escapade
[es′ kə pād′,
es′ kə pād′]
n. an adventure, especially one contrary to usual or proper behavior

expedition
[ek′ spi dish′ ən]
n. 1. a journey made for a specific purpose, such as exploration
2. the group of persons occupied in such a journey

fortitude
[fôr′ ti tōōd′]
n. mental and emotional strength in bravely facing challenges or danger

magnanimous
[mag nan′ ə məs]
adj. showing a noble spirit; unselfish; generous in forgiving

nomad
[nō′ mad]
n. 1. a wanderer
2. a member of a people with no set home who move in search of grazing land and food

peninsula
[pə nin′ sə lə]
n. an area of land almost fully surrounded by water except for a narrow strip of land connecting it with the mainland

plateau
[pla tō′]
n. 1. a land area having a fairly level surface elevated above adjoining land; a tableland
2. a period with little or no change; a stable state

pristine
[pris′ tēn, pri stēn′]
adj. unspoiled; pure; uncorrupted

terrain
[tə rān′]
n. an area of land, especially in reference to its natural features

WORDS TO WATCH

Which words would you like to practice with a bit more? Pick 3–4 words to study and list them below. Write the word, its definition, and compose your own sentence using the word correctly. This extra practice could be the final touch to learning a word.

Word	Definition	Your Sentence
1.		
2.		
3.		
4.		

14 Speech

Tips for Any Occasion

Speeches come in various forms. You may need to inform, persuade, or entertain your audience. You may have had weeks or months to prepare, or you may have to give an **impromptu** speech with little or no time to gather your thoughts. You could
5 give a speech to ten good friends or before thousands of strangers. You might be asked to speak at a wedding or a board meeting. The following are some tips you can use for any kind of speaking engagement.

If it is appropriate to your topic and audience, using **levity**
10 to begin a speech can help you and your audience to relax. By telling a joke or an amusing **anecdote,** you may find that you win your audience over in the first few minutes. People enjoy hearing stories, and when the stories are about the speaker, they can be particularly effective.
15 As you plan your speech, make sure your examples are **relevant** to your topic. You should use examples that deal with the subject you are talking about. For example, if your speech is on pollution, you will want to give examples of how bad the water supply is or how poor the air quality has become, not tell how you burned a casserole last night. Also, make sure that you check the
20 **verity** of any statements you make. You want to be accurate in what you say.

Another way to support your statements is by using expert **testimony.** Find people who are authorities on your topic, and quote them to back up your views. Before you use those people as sources, find out what their credentials are and whether other people in the profession respect them.

Think about the **ramifications** of your statements. What impact will your comments have on your
25 listeners? Also beware of making **derogatory** statements. You shouldn't belittle your listeners or make negative statements about gender, race, or other characteristics.

A technique that can make your speech vivid is **visualization.** Use words that will help listeners see what you are talking about. Describe the people and places that are important to your speech by using sensory details. Tell how something sounded, smelled, or tasted.
30 Lastly, don't forget a **summation** that covers your main points. Remember that your closing is your last chance to reach your audience. If there is something you want them to remember, tell them once again. Give your speech a sense of conclusion. Don't leave your audience feeling that something is missing.

Using these simple techniques can help you feel more confident any time you are asked to step up
35 to the podium.

░▓▓▓ PREDICTING

For each set, write the definition on the line next to the word to which it belongs. If you are unsure, return to the reading on page 88, and underline any context clues you find. After you've made your predictions, check your answers against the Word List on page 93. Place a checkmark in the box next to each word whose definition you missed. These are the words you'll want to study closely.

SET ONE

to-the-point	a short account	spontaneous
the quality of being real or correct	lightness	

☐   1. **impromptu** (line 3) _____

☐   2. **levity** (line 9) _____

☐   3. **anecdote** (line 11) _____

☐   4. **relevant** (line 16) _____

☐   5. **verity** (line 20) _____

SET TWO

proof	insulting	a concluding statement
developments	the formation of a mental image	

☐   6. **testimony** (line 21) _____

☐   7. **ramifications** (line 24) _____

☐   8. **derogatory** (line 25) _____

☐   9. **visualization** (line 27) _____

☐ 10. **summation** (line 30) _____

░▓▓▓ SELF-TESTS

1 Match each word with its synonym in Set One and its antonym in Set Two.

SYNONYMS

SET ONE

_____ 1. summation   a. image

_____ 2. testimony   b. result

_____ 3. visualization   c. addition

_____ 4. ramification   d. story

_____ 5. anecdote   e. proof

ANTONYMS

SET TWO

_____ 6. verity   f. supportive

_____ 7. levity   g. unrelated

_____ 8. relevant   h. seriousness

_____ 9. derogatory   i. planned

_____ 10. impromptu   j. untrue

2 Circle the word that correctly completes each sentence.

1. When I want to relax, I use (testimony, visualization) to picture myself sleeping in a meadow filled with flowers.

2. My sister told me a funny (ramification, anecdote) about trying to get her son to bed.

3. I have to give a(n) (impromptu, derogatory) speech tomorrow; I hope my instructor gives me a subject I know at least a little about.

4. We needed some (levity, testimony) in the room after Steve spent half an hour telling us about his gallbladder operation.

5. I got up and left the meeting when the speaker started to make (relevant, derogatory) statements about my college.

6. I wanted to believe the man's (anecdote, testimony), but the way he kept mumbling made me think he was lying.

7. In her (levity, summation), the mayor reviewed the major plans for the next year of her term.

8. I wasn't sure about the (ramification, verity) of the speaker's assertion that the moon is one hundred miles from the Earth.

9. I need to find a book on snakes because I think it will have (relevant, impromptu) examples for my talk on dangerous animals.

10. The (ramification, visualization) of arriving twenty minutes late didn't hit me until I looked at the timetable and saw that we would miss the ferry.

3 Use the vocabulary words to complete the following analogies. For instructions and practice, see Completing Analogies on page 6.

1. shopper : customer :: story : _____
2. complimentary : you have a beautiful home :: _____ : what an ugly house
3. bought a new sweater : purchase :: the sun is hot : _____
4. insult : anger :: joke : _____
5. escape : disappearance :: branching out : _____
6. exercise : take a long walk :: _____ : picture a sunny beach
7. unconnected : unrelated :: pertinent : _____
8. charity : I gave fifty dollars to the Cancer Society :: _____ : I saw him rob the bank
9. intended : planned :: _____ : spontaneous
10. first : last :: opening : _____

WORD WISE

Collocations

I seem to have *reached a plateau* in my weight loss; I have not gained or lost a pound in four weeks. (Chapter 13)

I love to camp in the interior of the park. It is a *pristine environment* because so few people make the effort to hike back here. (Chapter 13)

I couldn't stop myself from making a *derogatory remark* about Miranda's favorite football team once she had insulted my favorite team. (Chapter 14)

The outcome of the trial meant the success or failure of the company, so it was filled with *expert testimony* from people involved in all aspects of the business. (Chapter 14)

Word Pairs

Impromptu/Prepared: Impromptu (Chapter 14) means "not rehearsed; spontaneous." Prepared means "arranged; planned." I was forced to give an impromptu speech on "The Importance of Saving Money" for my speech class. I do much better on the prepared speeches when I have time to research and practice what I want to say.

Where Did It Come From?

Escapade (Chapter 13): comes from the Spanish *escapada* "a prank, flight, or escape." The root is *escapar* "to escape." The meaning "an adventure, especially one contrary to usual or proper behavior" shows elements of flight and escape from conventional rules.

Peninsula (Chapter 13): comes from the Latin *paeninsula* "almost an island." It is made from *paene* "almost" plus *insula* "island." The definition of "an area of land almost fully surrounded by water except for a narrow strip of land connecting it with the mainland" shows its "almost island" status.

Plateau (Chapter 13): comes from the French word *plateau*. In Old French the root was *platel* "a flat piece of metal, wood, etc.," which comes from *plat* "flat surface or thing." A plateau is "a land area having a level surface considerably raised above adjoining land."

INTERACTIVE EXERCISE

Pretend that you are preparing a speech on why the cafeteria needs better food. Make your answers to all but Question 10 deal with this topic.

1. Write an anecdote you could begin your speech with.

   _____

   _____

2. Give two examples that would be relevant to this topic.

   _____   _____

3. Who could give expert testimony on food?

   _____

4. Explain one way you could check on the verity of the manager's statement: "Providing healthy food is just too expensive for the cafeteria."

   _____

5. In using visualization, to which two senses would you want to appeal the most?

   _____   _____

6. How could you add levity to your talk?

   _____

7. What might be one ramification of your speech?

   _____

8. What type of derogatory statement should you avoid using?

   _____

9. Write a sentence that would be part of your summation.

   _____

10. If you had to give an impromptu talk about something, on what topic would you speak?

   _____

HINT

Meeting with a Study Group

To create an effective study session, keep these points in mind.

- Pick a place to meet that is beneficial for studying. You want a place where it's easy to talk, but where you won't be interrupted by telephones, children, or other distractions. Check on the availability of group study rooms in the library.
- Bring the necessary books, notes, and other materials to each session.
- Ask various group members to be "the expert" on different chapters or areas of study— have them share their in-depth study with the other group members. Give everyone a chance to participate and respect each person's views.
- Assign someone to keep the group on track and be aware of time limits. Gently remind people who start to talk about other topics that you are all there to study. Ask anyone to leave who does not really want to study.
- Evaluate how useful the study session was and decide what changes may be needed for the next time. Try to make the study sessions fun and productive.

WORD LIST

anecdote
[an' ik dōt']

n. 1. a short account of an interesting or humorous incident
2. secret particulars of history or biography

derogatory
[di rog' ə tôr' ē]

adj. offensive; insulting; critical

impromptu
[im promp' tōō]

adj. not rehearsed; spontaneous

levity
[lev' ə tē]

n. 1. lightness of speech or manner; frivolity
2. lightness; buoyancy
3. changeableness

ramification
[ram' ə fi kā' shən]

n. 1. a development growing out of and often complicating a problem, plan, or statement; a consequence
2. the act of branching out

relevant
[rel' ə vənt]

adj. pertinent; to-the-point

summation
[sə mā' shən]

n. 1. a concluding statement containing a summary of principal points
2. the act of totaling; addition

testimony
[tes' tə mō' nē]

n. evidence in support of a fact or assertion; proof

verity
[ver' ə tē]

n. 1. the quality of being real, accurate, or correct
2. a statement of principle considered to be permanent truth

visualization
[vizh' ōō ə li zā' shən]

n. the formation of a mental image or images

WORDS TO WATCH

Which words would you like to practice with a bit more? Pick 3–5 words to study and list them below. Write the word, its definition, and compose your own sentence using the word correctly. This extra practice could be the final touch to learning a word.

Word	Definition	Your Sentence
1.		
2.		
3.		
4.		
5.		

15

Word Parts II

Look for words with these **prefixes, roots,** and/or **suffixes** as you work through this book. You may have already seen some of them, and you will see others in later chapters. Learning basic word parts can help you figure out the meanings of unfamiliar words.

prefix: a word part added to the beginning of a word that changes the meaning of the root
root: a word's basic part with its essential meaning
suffix: a word part added to the end of a word; indicates the part of speech

WORD PART	MEANING	EXAMPLES AND DEFINITIONS
Prefixes		
bi-	two	*biannual:* happening twice each year *bicycle:* a vehicle with two wheels
mono-	one	*monopoly:* control by one group *monolith:* one block of stone
prot-	first, primary	*protagonist:* the leading or primary figure *protein:* molecules making up a primary part of every life-form
tri-	three	*triumvirate:* rule by three people *triangle:* a figure with three sides
Roots		
-flu-, -flux-	to flow	*influx:* an act of flowing in *superfluous:* overflowing; excessive
-her-, -hes-	to stick	*coherent:* sticking to one point *adherent:* a person who sticks to a belief
-plac-	to please	*placate:* to please; to calm *placid:* pleasantly calm
-port-	to carry	*portfolio:* a case for carrying papers or drawings *portable:* easy to carry
-sta-, -sti-	to stand, to be in a place	*status:* standing; social position *destitute:* lacking; without support or standing

Suffixes

-ade (makes a noun)	action or process	*escapade:* the action of a reckless adventure *promenade:* the process of taking a walk
-most (makes an adjective)	most	*utmost:* the most extreme *foremost:* the most important
-phobia (makes a noun)	fear of	*acrophobia:* a fear of heights *claustrophobia:* a fear of enclosed places

▌▌▌▌▌ SELF-TESTS

1 Read each definition and choose the appropriate word. Use each word once. The meaning of the word part is underlined to help you make the connection. Refer to the Word Parts list if you need help.

1. of an eyeglass, having <u>two</u> portions _____

2. <u>pleased</u> with oneself often without an awareness of some problem _____

3. a substance that is capable of <u>flowing</u> _____

4. <u>sticking</u> to <u>one</u> point _____

5. a vocal utterance in <u>one</u> unvaried sound _____

6. the <u>action</u> of obstructing passage or progress _____

7. a <u>fear of</u> people _____

8. <u>to carry</u> out of a country _____

9. a series of <u>three</u> plays, novels, movies, etc. _____

10. <u>standing</u> still; not moving _____

VOCABULARY LIST

trilogy	fluid
blockade	complacent
bifocal	monotone
export	coherent
anthrophobia	stationary

2 Finish the sentences with the meaning of each word part. Use each meaning once. The word part is underlined to help you make the connection.

VOCABULARY LIST

pleased	two	one	first	stick
flow	most	stand	fear of	to carry

1. We have <u>bi</u>monthly meetings; it is good to get together and talk every _____ months.

2. Currently in American society, <u>mono</u>gamy is the law. People seem to feel that it is better to have _____ spouse at a time.

3. Anthony is <u>flu</u>ent in five languages. The ability to speak another language just seems to _____ out of him.

4. My great-grandfather was a <u>proto</u>martyr in the fight for safe working conditions for miners. In his town, he was the _____ person to die in a riot caused by a strike.

5. To placate the hungry guests, June gave them some cheese and crackers to keep them _____ before the main course was ready.

6. I did not know Tina suffered from ailurophobia until Seeley jumped on her lap and she confessed to a _____ cats.

7. The adhesive tape really helped my package _____ together. My sister said it took her an hour to get it open.

8. I reveal my innermost secrets to my diary. I don't dare share my _____ secret feelings with anyone.

9. I asked the porter at the train station _____ my bags to my car because I was tired of lifting them.

10. I am not going to let any obstacles (financial, emotional, or time-consuming) _____ in the way of my completing college.

3 Finish the story using the word parts found below. Use each word part once. Your knowledge of word parts, as well as the context clues, will help you create the correct words. If you do not understand the meaning of a word you have made, check the dictionary for the definition or to see whether the word exists.

WORD PARTS LIST

her	tri	plac	sti	bi
mono	most	flu	port	phobia

AN EXCITING JOB

I work for a business that im ⁽¹⁾_____s furniture from around the world. The main offices are in New York and Los Angeles, so I have become ⁽¹⁾_____coastal with apartments in both cities. I am ⁽³⁾_____lingual: I speak English, Chinese, and Spanish. I am sent to several countries around the world. At first this was a problem for me because I suffered from aero ⁽⁴⁾_____. I hated to fly. I overcame my fear because I wanted to see the world. I am a strong ad ⁽⁵⁾_____ent of the benefits of travel to make one more understanding of cultural

differences. It is fascinating to see the in ⁽⁶⁾_____ence countries have had on one another. The world is not a ⁽⁷⁾_____id place; changes are occurring everywhere. Some people are ob ⁽⁸⁾_____nate and want time to stand still, but it won't. I am excited by the new things I

see, and no one country has a __(9)_____poly on the biggest or best of anything. The

northern__(10)_____ point I have been to is Hammerfest, Norway. It certainly was cold there,

but I picked up some gorgeous tables and chairs.

4 Pick the best definition for each underlined word using your knowledge of word parts. Circle the word
part in each of the underlined words.

a. able to speak two languages

b. conduct; how one carries oneself

c. tending to unify or stick together

d. sweetly or smoothly flowing

e. not to be pacified or pleased

f. three children born at the same time

g. stale or foul from standing, as in a
pool of water

h. the action of a pouring out of anything

i. an abnormal fear of being alone

j. an original draft from which a
document is prepared

_____ 1. Because our dog has <u>monophobia</u>, we have to take her with us everywhere.

_____ 2. My cousin Sarah was shocked and pleased when she had <u>triplets</u>: two girls and a boy.

_____ 3. The secretary used the <u>protocol</u> to prepare the treaty for the next day's meeting.

_____ 4. I was proud of my son's <u>deportment</u> at the luncheon. He is usually loud, but he was quiet
and well mannered.

_____ 5. The president had to face a <u>fusillade</u> of questions from reporters about his actions after it
was discovered that he had been hiding money in a secret account.

_____ 6. I decided to major in international business because I like working with others, and I knew
that my <u>bilingual</u> skills would help me get a job overseas.

_____ 7. The <u>stagnant</u> pond had a horrible smell to it.

_____ 8. The singer's <u>mellifluous</u> voice kept the audience enchanted for two hours.

_____ 9. Because of the movie's <u>cohesive</u> structure, it was easy to understand how the different
characters all came to know each other.

_____ 10. The little boy was <u>implacable</u>; nothing would quiet him until his mother stopped at the toy
store.

5 A good way to remember word parts is to pick one word that uses a word part and understand how that
word part functions in the word. Then you can apply that meaning to other words that have the same
word part. Use the words to help you match the word part to its meaning.

SET ONE

_____ 1. **bi-:** biannual, bicycle, binocular

_____ 2. **-flu-, -flux-:** fluid, influx, fluctuation

_____ 3. **-sta-, -sti-:** status, static, stationary

_____ 4. **-most:** utmost, foremost, southernmost

_____ 5. **-plac-:** placate, placid, placebo

a. to flow

b. to please

c. two

d. to stand, to be in a place

e. most

_____	6. **mono-:** monolith, monopoly, monotone	f. fear of
_____	7. **-port-:** portfolio, portable, import	g. to carry
_____	8. **-ade:** escapade, blockade, promenade	h. one
_____	9. **-her-, -hes-:** coherent, inherent, adhesive	i. action or process
_____	10. **-phobia:** acrophobia, metrophobia, numerophobia	j. to stick

WORD WISE

Word Groups

Putting words into related groups can be a way to help your mind organize new vocabulary. To create word groups get a piece of paper, pick a category, and list as many of the vocabulary words whose definitions fit under that heading in a general way. You will, of course, need to know the shades of meaning the more frequently you use a word. The academic subjects used in each chapter of this book are already one way to organize some of the words. You will want to come up with other categories as you study words from multiple chapters. For example, here are four words to begin a sample list of eight vocabulary words that fit the category of "the arts": cinematography (Chapter 1), repertoire (Chapter 2), and amphitheater and limelight (Chapter 9). As you work through the book, look for four other words that would fit this category and return here to complete the list.

1. _____
2. _____
3. _____
4. _____

Other possible categories are "science words," "business words," "qualities a person would want to have," and "undesirable characteristics." For a fun and collaborative way to use word groups see the directions for Category Race in Chapter 20.

HINT

Campus Resources

Most colleges provide services to enhance your educational experience: learn to use these resources. Look into writing centers, computer labs, and tutoring programs for help as you prepare papers or study for tests. If you encounter any problems, consider the benefits of contacting counseling, disabled student services, or the financial aid office. You might also want to check into whether your campus offers any child-care facilities. Check your instructors' office hours and find their offices. Asking questions outside of class or getting help with papers during office hours are great ways to improve your learning. The faculty and staff on campus are there for you. Taking the time to find out where campus resources are located and what hours they are open can make your college experience more rewarding.

Use the dictionary to find a word you don't know that uses each word part listed below. Write the meaning of the word part, the word, and the definition. If your dictionary has the etymology (history) of the word, see how the word part relates to the meaning, and write the etymology after the definition.

Word Part	Meaning	Word	Definition and Etymology
EXAMPLE:			
bi-	two	bicorn	having two horns or hornlike parts. Latin bicornis; bi- two + -corn having a horn
1. -sta-			
2. mono-			
3. -port-			
4. prot-			
5. tri-			

16 Literature

Look Deeply

Poetry is an enduring form of literature because it touches people's hearts and minds as it deals with universal themes, such as love, death, and nature. However, many people also suffer from **metrophobia**, a fear of poetry. What often scares people about
5 poetry is its **ambiguous** nature. A poem doesn't always have one clear meaning. It can have several possible meanings, which can be intimidating, but it can also be the joy of poetry because it can be discussed, delighted in, and reflected on in numerous ways.

    The **foremost** Scottish poet Robert "Bobby" Burns
10 (1759–1796) shows how the theme of love can be imaginatively dealt with in verse in his poem "A Red, Red Rose." He wrote:

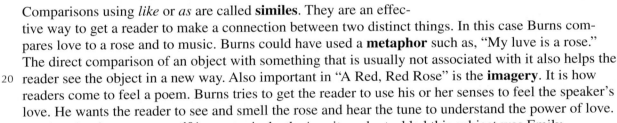

> O My Luve's like a red, red rose,
>   That's newly sprung in June;
> O My Luve's like the melodie
15   That's sweetly played in tune.

Comparisons using *like* or *as* are called **similes**. They are an effective way to get a reader to make a connection between two distinct things. In this case Burns compares love to a rose and to music. Burns could have used a **metaphor** such as, "My luve is a rose." The direct comparison of an object with something that is usually not associated with it also helps the
20 reader see the object in a new way. Also important in "A Red, Red Rose" is the **imagery**. It is how readers come to feel a poem. Burns tries to get the reader to use his or her senses to feel the speaker's love. He wants the reader to see and smell the rose and hear the tune to understand the power of love.

    Another important **motif** in poetry is death. A writer who tackled this subject was Emily Dickinson (1830–1886). Dickinson was a recluse who rarely saw anyone for most of her life. All but
25 seven of her almost fifteen hundred poems were published **posthumously**. In her poem "Because I Could Not Stop for Death" she uses **personification** by giving death a carriage in which to pick up the speaker: "He [Death] kindly stopped for me—/The carriage held but just Ourselves." Giving an inanimate object human characteristics can help a reader identify with the subject of the poem.

    To overcome one's metrophobia it is important to appreciate that it is often through **inference** that
30 readers come to understand a poem. Poets don't always come right out and tell the reader what they mean. For instance, in her poem "A Song in the Front Yard" American poet Gwendolyn Brooks (1917–2000) seems to be talking about her yard:

> I've stayed in the front yard all my life.
> I want a peek at the back
35 Where it's rough and untended and hungry weed grows.
> A girl gets sick of a rose.

The reader now has to be willing to do some reasoning to figure out possible meanings. The front yard certainly seems to mean more than just a yard, but what does it mean? The rose and all its connotations faces the reader again, and he or she needs to decide what it stands for this time. Though
40 carefully looking at a poem can be challenging because of the language or format used, it is this effort to understand that makes poetry so enriching for readers.

▐▐▐▌ PREDICTING

For each set, write the definition on the line next to the word to which it belongs. If you are unsure, return to the reading on page 100, and underline any context clues you find. After you've made your predictions, check your answers against the Word List on page 105. Place a checkmark in the box next to each word whose definition you missed. These are the words you'll want to study closely.

SET ONE

first in importance	a fear of poetry	open to several possible meanings
comparisons using *like* or *as*		a comparison between things that are not literally alike

❑   1. **metrophobia** (line 4) _____

❑   2. **ambiguous** (line 5) _____

❑   3. **foremost** (line 9) _____

❑   4. **similes** (line 16) _____

❑   5. **metaphor** (line 18) _____

SET TWO

the dominant theme in a work of art	mental images	occurring after death
the act of drawing a conclusion		the act of giving inanimate objects human qualities

❑   6. **imagery** (line 20) _____

❑   7. **motif** (line 23) _____

❑   8. **posthumously** (line 25) _____

❑   9. **personification** (line 26) _____

❑   10. **inference** (line 29) _____

▐▐▐▌ SELF-TESTS

1   Circle the correct meaning of each vocabulary word.

1. posthumously: occurring before birth   occurring after death

2. imagery: mental images   real items

3. metrophobia: a love of poetry   a fear of poetry

4. metaphor: a comparison using *like* or *as*   a direct comparison

5. ambiguous: unclear   clear

6. inference: making a wild guess   drawing a conclusion from evidence

7. foremost: least   leading

8. personification: person without any good qualities   a person that is the perfect example of a quality

9. motif: a recurring element   an element used once

10. simile: a comparison using *like* or *as*   a direct comparison

2 Match each word to the appropriate example.

VOCABULARY LIST

foremost	simile	imagery	ambiguous	metrophobia
inference	motifs	metaphor	posthumously	personification

1. His smile is a bolt of lightning. _____
2. Her first novel was printed fifty years after her death. _____
3. "I'm afraid to read Whitman's poem *Leaves of Grass*." _____
4. The tree's branches spread over me like a fortress. _____
5. The walls shook with laughter, the ceiling had a wide grin, and the floors just smiled; the house knew my cleaning wouldn't last a day. _____
6. I bit into the large, cream-cheese frosted, freshly baked cinnamon roll; listened to the screams from the midway rides; and felt the warm sun on my back—it was good to be at the county fair.
_____
7. Yesterday was the change to daylight saving time, and John is an hour late; he probably didn't change his clock. _____
8. Nature's beauty, lost love, and patriotism are a few common ones. _____
9. The unexpected phone message: "Pick me up at the airport at 8 tomorrow." _____
10. William Shakespeare as a playwright and poet, and Beethoven in music. _____

3 Finish the sentences using the vocabulary words. Use each word once.

VOCABULARY LIST

metrophobia	ambiguous	imagery	simile	foremost
personification	metaphor	motif	inference	posthumously

1. Kafka didn't want his writing published _____, so he asked his friend to destroy all of his remaining work.
2. Time is an important _____ in many of Edgar Allan Poe's works.

3. The main character's answer about where he had been last night was _____ . Without a clear explanation of his activities, he became a prime suspect in the inspector's investigation of the murder.

4. In "A Birthday" Christina Rossetti writes, "My heart is like an apple tree/Whose boughs are bent with thick set fruit." The _____ shows how happy the speaker is because she has found love.

5. My friend compared himself to a battleship. That _____ fits him because he loves conflict.

6. Robert Frost is one of the _____ American poets.

7. William Carlos Williams uses _____ to help the reader see the wheelbarrow. He describes it as being red and "glazed with rain/water/beside the white/chickens."

8. *The Wonderful Wizard of Oz* uses _____ when the tree yells at Dorothy for picking one of its apples.

9. When the woman in the story said her husband wouldn't be coming to dinner, the reader had to make a(n) _____ because no direct reason for his disappearance was given.

10. Because some poets use many historical and literary references, their poems can be hard to understand, which has led to _____ for many people.

WORD WISE

Context Clue Mini-Lesson 5

This lesson combines the techniques you have practiced in the four previous context clue mini-lessons. You will be looking for synonyms, antonyms, examples, and general meaning to help you understand the underlined words. In the paragraph below, circle any clues you find and then write the types of clues and your definitions on the lines next to the words that follow the paragraph.

The severe winter weather had kept me inside for the last three weeks. In the last few days the storms had become sporadic. Since the snowfall was no longer constant, I thought I had a chance to get out. I came up with the preposterous idea of walking to my friend's house four miles away. It was ridiculous to think that I could get that far in the cold with snow still covering much of the area, but I headed out. For the first few blocks I savored the smell of the fresh air and the beauty of the snow-covered trees. But after another two blocks, the snow returned, and I quickly turned around.

Type of Context Clue and Your Definition

1. Severe _____

2. Sporadic _____

3. Preposterous _____

4. Savored _____

Write a poem about love or death using four of the following elements: imagery, metaphor, motif, personification, or simile. Don't let metrophobia get in the way. You don't have to write a great poem; this is just a chance to practice using the vocabulary words.

_____

_____

_____

_____

_____

_____

_____

_____

_____

_____

_____

_____

_____

_____

HINT

Tips for Enjoying Literature

Readers enjoy a book more when they become involved with it. Try to put yourself in a novel or short story by imagining yourself in a character's situation. What would you do if you had to stop an alien invasion, cope with a broken heart, or solve a murder? Learn to appreciate the descriptions of the places in the story. Try to visualize yourself hiking through the jungle, cooking a big meal in the kitchen, or hiding under a bed. Look for the author's message as you read. Ask yourself what point the author is trying to get across. Do you agree or disagree with the author's point? By putting yourself in a work of literature and thinking about the significance of events, you will want to keep reading to see what happens to the characters because now they and their world are a part of you.

ambiguous
[am big′ yoo əs]

adj. 1. open to several possible meanings or interpretations
2. difficult to understand; unclear; indistinct

foremost
[fôr′ mōst]

adj. first in importance, place, or time; chief

imagery
[im′ ij rē]

n. 1. the use of vivid descriptions to make mental images or pictures
2. mental images

inference
[in′ fər əns]

n. the act of drawing a conclusion from evidence

metaphor
[met′ ə fôr′, -fər′]

n. a figure of speech that makes a comparison between things that are not literally alike

metrophobia
[me′ trə fō′ bē ə, mē′-]

n. a fear of poetry

motif
[mō tēf′]

n. the dominant theme in a literary or musical composition; a recurring element in a work of art

personification
[pər son′ ə fi kā′ shən]

n. 1. the act of giving human qualities to inanimate objects or abstract ideas
2. a person or thing that is the perfect example of a quality

posthumously
[pos′ choo məs lē]

adv. 1. occurring after death
2. published after the death of the author

simile
[sim′ ə lē]

n. a figure of speech that compares two unlike things, introduced by the word *like* or *as*

▐▐▐▌ WORDS TO WATCH

Which words would you like to practice with a bit more? Pick 3–5 words to study and list them below. Write the word, its definition, and compose your own sentence using the word correctly. This extra practice could be the final touch to learning a word.

	Word	Definition	Your Sentence
1.	_____	_____	_____
2.	_____	_____	_____
3.	_____	_____	_____
4.	_____	_____	_____
5.	_____	_____	_____

CHAPTER

17 Art History

The European Gallery

Joseph Turner
British 1775–1851
Burning of the Houses of Parliament
watercolor 1843

Joseph Mallord William Turner (1775–1851), *Burning of the Houses of Parliament*, 1843. Watercolor. Copyright Clore Collection, Tate Gallery, London/Art Resource, NY

5 Turner captures the **essence** of the fire through the various **hues.** The red, orange, and yellow colors convey the heat of the fire, while the darker colors are **evocative** of the smoke. Turner skillfully uses light and dark to suggest different elements. The whole painting is
10 **emblematic** of the fire without directly showing it.

El Greco (Domenikos Theotokópoulos)
Spanish (b. Crete) 1541–1614
View and Map of Toledo
oil on canvas c. 1610–1614

El Greco (Domenikos Theotokópoulos) (1541–1613), *View and Map of Toledo.* Canvas, 132 × 228 cm. Casa y Museo del Greco, Toledo, Spain. Copyright Erich Lessing/Art Resource, NY

15 El Greco's limited color **spectrum** gives the painting a somewhat somber quality. The severity of the scene, however, is offset by his use of **perspective** that causes the eye to move from the foreground figures to the Virgin and angels in the sky. The dramatic clouds and floating
20 figures give energy to what could be considered an **austere** painting.

Vincent van Gogh
Dutch 1853–1890
Yellow Wheat and Cypresses
25 oil on canvas 1889

Vincent van Gogh (1853–1890), *Yellow Wheat and Cypresses,* 1889. Oil on canvas. National Gallery, London, Great Britain. Copyright Erich Lessing/Art Resource, NY

Van Gogh uses several colors in his **palette** to express the grandeur of nature. Van Gogh was extremely concerned with how colors convey certain moods. This **picturesque** scene draws the viewer into his multicolored, swirling world. **Eschewing** conventional techniques, van Gogh uses
30 thick brush strokes to make his scenes come alive.

▉▍▉▍ PREDICTING

For each set, write the definition on the line next to the word to which it belongs. If you are unsure, return to the reading on page 106, and underline any context clues you find. After you've made your predictions, check your answers against the Word List on page 111. Place a checkmark in the box next to each word whose definition you missed. These are the words you'll want to study closely.

SET ONE

symbolic	colors	the crucial element	a range of related qualities	suggestive

❑ 1. **essence** (line 5) _____

❑ 2. **hues** (line 6) _____

❑ 3. **evocative** (line 7) _____

❑ 4. **emblematic** (line 10) _____

❑ 5. **spectrum** (line 15) _____

SET TWO

charming	avoiding	severe	range of colors used in a painting

techniques for representing three-dimensional objects on a two-dimensional surface

❑ 6. **perspective** (line 17) _____

❑ 7. **austere** (line 21) _____

❑ 8. **palette** (line 26) _____

❑ 9. **picturesque** (line 28) _____

❑ 10. **eschewing** (line 30) _____

▉▍▉▍ SELF-TESTS

1 Put a T for true or F for false next to each sentence.

_____ 1. Pink is an austere color.

_____ 2. A painting of garbage cans would probably be referred to as picturesque.

_____ 3. A person's perspective can change when he or she is given more information.

_____ 4. Flags are emblematic of a country.

_____ 5. Bell-bottom pants are evocative of the 1960s.

_____ 6. Most people would eschew the offer of a free plane ticket.

_____ 7. The essence of doing well in school is studying.

_____ 8. An artist's palette usually contains only black, white, and gray.

_____ 9. Most people like a spectrum of activities to choose from when on vacation.

_____ 10. A popular hue for buildings is lime green.

2 Complete the following quotations overheard in art museums around the world. Use each word once.

VOCABULARY LIST

emblematic	essence	hues	perspective	spectrum
austere	eschew	evocative	palette	picturesque

1. "Rembrandt's paintings are too _____ for me; the man needs to lighten up."

2. "In her glorious flower paintings, O'Keeffe effectively uses her _____ to present the rich colors of nature."

3. "Diego Rivera's mural gave me a better _____ on the struggles in Mexico."

4. "I like the _____ quality of Georges Seurat's painting of people relaxing in the park on a Sunday afternoon. The pointillist technique and the colors make it an interesting and charming work."

5. "I know Picasso was trying to _____ traditional forms in his paintings, but I cannot see a woman coming down that staircase."

6. "The African mask exhibit was _____ of how we often hide who we are."

7. "Dali's paintings really capture the _____ of the dreamworld."

8. "The pink and purple _____ in Suzanne Valadon's *Lilacs and Peonies* show the delicacy of spring."

9. "I appreciate the _____ of works in the modern art section; there is everything from a Warhol painting to a huge plastic banana."

10. "I found the Hiroshige print of the rain shower to be quite _____; I could feel myself in a downpour."

Georgia O'Keeffe (1887–1986), *White Flower on Red Earth, #1*, 1943. Oil on canvas, 26 in. × 30 1/4 in. Collection of the Newark Museum, Newark, New Jersey. Copyright The Newark Museum/Art Resource, NY. © 2002 The Georgia O'Keeffe Foundation/Artists Rights Society (ARS), New York

Georges Seurat (French, 1859–1891), *A Sunday on La Grande Jatte,* 1884–1886. Oil on canvas, 207.6 × 308 cm. Helen Birch Bartlett Memorial Collection, The Art Institute of Chicago. 1926.224. Photograph © 2001, The Art Institute of Chicago. All Rights Reserved.

3 In each group, circle the word that does not have a connection to the other three words. See Chapter 11 for an example.

1. symbolic   direct   emblematic   representative

2. edge   spirit   essence   core

3. hue   color   tint   bare

4. variety   range   sameness   spectrum

5. palette   board   range   singular

6. eschew   avoid   escape   join

7. elaborate   austere   stern   simple

8. vivid   charming   ugly   picturesque

9. view   indifferent   perspective   attitude

10. evocative   suggestive   summon   stated

WORD WISE

Collaborative Activity: The Story Behind the Picture

Equipment needed: Paper, pens, and pictures (postcards, family photographs, ads, or pictures from magazines)

This activity is good for visual learners and for those who like to write. It can be done in groups of three to four people or individually. Each small group selects a picture from the ones people have brought. The group writes a short (one to two paragraph) story for the picture. Use four to six of the vocabulary words you are studying in the story. If you are doing the activity individually, write your own story using four to six of the vocabulary words in the story. Share the picture and story with the other groups. After the sharing, choose another picture and play another round. After two or three rounds, discuss how the same picture produces different stories.

You are an art critic. Use seven of the vocabulary words to write a column about Claude Monet's painting *White Waterlilies*.

Claude Monet (1840–1926), *White Waterlilies,* Pushkin Museum of Fine Arts, Moscow. Copyright Scala/Art Resource, NY

HINT

Make It Yours

An important step in learning new vocabulary is to practice using the words. When you feel comfortable with a word's definition, start using the word in your writing and conversations. If you only try to memorize the word for a test, you will likely forget it after the test. Make your acquisition of new vocabulary meaningful by using the words in everyday situations. Also try to connect the word to prior knowledge or experiences. Are there situations you have been in in which the word would be appropriate? Try to integrate the word with your life as much as possible. You will impress your friends and family and feel good about yourself as you show people what you have learned.

austere
[ô stēr']
adj. 1. severe or stern; somber
2. simple; bare

emblematic
[em' blə mat' ik]
adj. serving as an emblem; symbolic; representative

eschew
[es chōō']
v. to avoid; to shun; to escape

essence
[es' əns]
n. the quality of a thing that gives it its identity; the crucial element; core

evocative
[i vok' ə tiv]
adj. having the power to produce a reaction; suggestive

hue
[hyōō]
n. 1. color; tint; shade
2. character; aspect

palette
[pal' it]
n. 1. the range of colors used in a particular painting or by a particular artist
2. a board on which an artist mixes paints

perspective
[pər spek' tiv]
n. 1. any of various techniques for representing three-dimensional objects and depth relationships on a two-dimensional surface
2. a view
3. a point of view; attitude

picturesque
[pik' chə resk']
adj. 1. charming; interesting in an unusual way; vivid
2. suitable for a picture

spectrum
[spek' trəm]
n. a range of related qualities, ideas, or activities; variety

▮▮▮ WORDS TO WATCH

Which words would you like to practice with a bit more? Pick 3–5 words to study and list them below. Write the word, its definition, and compose your own sentence using the word correctly. This extra practice could be the final touch to learning a word.

Word	Definition	Your Sentence
1. _____	_____	_____
2. _____	_____	_____
3. _____	_____	_____
4. _____	_____	_____
5. _____	_____	_____

18 Foreign Languages

Creeping into English

More foreign words and phrases creep into common English usage each year. Because English has always borrowed words from other languages, people aren't always aware that a word originated in another country. For example, *banana* and *zombie* are African words, *cookie* and *yacht* come from the Dutch, and *yogurt* from Turkish. Other words still sound foreign, but they are used every day when
5 speaking English.

Imagine eating dinner **alfresco** on a pleasant evening. While you are enjoying the outdoors, your waiter comes to tell you about the soup **du jour** and other daily specials. After you take a sip of the delicious French onion soup you ordered, you sit back and enjoy a **bon mot** your companion has just uttered. As you smile at his witty remark, you think, "I'm living **la dolce vita** as I take pleasure in my
10 excellent meal, good company, and lovely atmosphere." **Voilà!** Possibly without even being aware of it, you have just spent an evening relying on foreign phrases.

Foreign words also appear frequently in the media. The Latin phrase **carpe diem** was an important message in the film *Dead Poet's Society,* and the words appear on numerous calendars and motivational posters. To seize the day is a message we often forget in today's hectic world. The term
15 **doppelgänger** comes from German for a ghostly double, and the concept has been explored in works by writers such as Edgar Allan Poe and Robert Louis Stevenson. Even a single word can have an impact in a story, such as **nada** as used in "A Clean Well-Lighted Place" by Ernest Hemingway. Nothing can certainly come to mean something.

It isn't necessarily a **faux pas** to not understand every foreign word or phrase currently in use, but
20 to avoid possibly embarrassing moments the wise person will want to learn these phrases. The multicultural **zeitgeist** of the twenty-first century asks all of us to grow along with the language.

▌▌▌▌▌ PREDICTING

For each set, write the definition on the line next to the word to which it belongs. If you are unsure, return to the reading on page 112, and underline any context clues you find. After you've made your predictions, check your answers against the Word List on page 117. Place a checkmark in the box next to each word whose definition you missed. These are the words you'll want to study closely.

SET ONE

There it is!	a witty remark	out-of-doors	the good life	as served on a particular day

- ❑ 1. **alfresco** (line 6) _____
- ❑ 2. **du jour** (line 7) _____
- ❑ 3. **bon mot** (line 8) _____
- ❑ 4. **la dolce vita** (line 9) _____
- ❑ 5. **voilà** (line 10) _____

SET TWO

nothing	the spirit of the time	seize the day	a mistake	a ghostly double or counterpart

- ❑ 6. **carpe diem** (line 12) _____
- ❑ 7. **doppelgänger** (line 15) _____
- ❑ 8. **nada** (line 17) _____
- ❑ 9. **faux pas** (line 19) _____
- ❑ 10. **zeitgeist** (line 21) _____

▌▌▌▌▌ SELF-TESTS

Match each word with its synonym in Set One and its antonym in Set Two.

1 SYNONYMS
SET ONE

_____ 1. carpe diem   a. mood

_____ 2. doppelgänger b. mistake

_____ 3. bon mot   c. grab the chance

_____ 4. zeitgeist   d. double

_____ 5. faux pas   e. witticism

ANTONYMS

SET TWO

_____ 6. alfresco   f. old

_____ 7. nada   g. Darn!

_____ 8. la dolce vita   h. indoors

_____ 9. voilà   i. everything

_____ 10. du jour   j. dullness

2 Finish the sentences using the vocabulary words. Use each word once.

VOCABULARY LIST

bon mot	nada	alfresco	dolce vita	doppelgänger
carpe diem	voilà	faux pas	zeitgeist	du jour

1. The special _____ at the cafeteria was kidney pie; I decided to pass.
2. As we sat on the porch of our cabin overlooking the lake, we thought this was the _____.
3. Edgar Allan Poe has a scary story about a man who meets his _____ at a party.
4. My cousin is the expert at the _____; she always knows the right thing to say to make people laugh.
5. After a busy semester, I was looking forward to doing _____ for a week.
6. Sometimes I get so involved in everything I need to get done that I forget to _____.
7. I think that having toilet paper stuck to one's shoe all night would be considered a(n) _____ at most parties.
8. In the 1920s the _____ seemed to be to party as much as possible in order to forget World War I.
9. The play will be performed _____ to enhance the play's forest setting.
10. I kept trying, and, _____, my story was finally accepted for publication.

3 Connect the vocabulary words to the following items or situations. Use each word once.

VOCABULARY LIST

alfresco	carpe diem	du jour	doppelgänger	voilà
bon mot	faux pas	la dolce vita	nada	zeitgeist

1. a pocket without any lira, pesos, or francs _____
2. French onion soup _____
3. greed in the 1980s _____
4. under the stars _____

5. "There is only one thing in the world worse than being talked about, and that is not being talked about."—Oscar Wilde _____

6. I found my keys! _____

7. asking a woman whether her child is her grandchild _____

8. When the woman he has admired all semester asks to borrow a pen, the young man asks her out. _____

9. Robert Louis Stevenson's character Markheim meets his evil self. _____

10. a three-course lunch followed by a nap _____

WORD WISE

Collocations

The award had to be *given posthumously* because the ambassador died in a plane crash on her most recent peace-saving mission. (Chapter 16)

I have a *better perspective* on my problem since I took last night to think about it. (Chapter 17)

For Sue the *essence of* a good meal is having good friends to share it with. (Chapter 17)

I like to eat out on Fridays because the *soup du jour* is usually clam chowder. (Chapter 18)

Word Pairs

Metaphor/Simile: Metaphor (Chapter 16) means "a figure of speech that makes a comparison between things that are not literally alike." A simile (Chapter 16) means "a figure of speech that compares two unlike things, introduced by the word *like* or *as*." The poet uses both a metaphor ("her eyes are diamonds") and a simile ("her cheeks are like apples") to describe the woman.

Where Did It Come From?

Doppelgänger (Chapter 18): comes from the German *doppel* "double" and *gänger* "goer or walker." The meaning of doppelgänger is "a ghostly double or counterpart of a living person." There is a theory that a person's double is somewhere out there. Famous people from Percy Shelley to Goethe have reported seeing their doppelgänger. The doppelgänger theme is popular in literature and film from Guy de Maupassant's short story "Lui" to the film *The Man with My Face*.

Pretend you have enrolled in a Semester Abroad program, and write a letter to a friend telling about your adventures overseas. Use at least seven of the vocabulary words in your note.

HINT

Working with Others

When working with others, keep these points in mind:

- Be aware of time limits.
- Give everyone a chance to participate.
- Discover each person's strengths.
- Respect each person's views.
- Have fun.

alfresco [al fres′ kō]	Italian.	*adv.*	out-of-doors; in the open air
		adj.	outdoor
bon mot [bôn mō′]	French.	*n.*	a witty remark or comment; witticism
carpe diem [kär′ pe dē′ em, kär′ pä dē′ əm]	Latin.	*n.*	seize the day; enjoy the present
dolce vita [dôl′ che vē′ tä]	Italian.	*n.*	the good life (usually preceded by *la*)
doppelgänger [dop′ əl gang′ ər]	German.	*n.*	a ghostly double or counterpart of a living person

du jour [də zhoor′, doo-]	French.	*adj.*	1. as prepared or served on a particular day 2. fashionable; current
faux pas [fō pä′]	French.	*n.*	a mistake; a slip or blunder in manners or conduct; an embarrassing social error
nada [nä′ dä]	Spanish.	*n.*	nothing
voilà [vwä lä′]	French.	*interj.*	There it is! (used to express success or satisfaction)
zeitgeist [tsīt′ gīst′]	German.	*n.*	the spirit of the time; the general feeling of a particular period of time

▬▬▬ WORDS TO WATCH

Which words would you like to practice with a bit more? Pick 3–5 words to study and list them below. Write the word, its definition, and compose your own sentence using the word correctly. This extra practice could be the final touch to learning a word.

	Word	Definition	Your Sentence
1.	_____	_____	_____
2.	_____	_____	_____
3.	_____	_____	_____
4.	_____	_____	_____
5.	_____	_____	_____

19 Biology

A Walk in the Woods

Welcome to the Small Woods Nature Trail!

By using this guide you will learn about the **flora** and **fauna** of the area. A variety of plants and animals live in the woods and interact with each other in order to survive. Look for the numbered signposts that correspond with this guide. Enjoy our **sojourn** through the **myriad** wonders of nature!

Stop 1 In front of you is an example of a **parasitic** relationship. The mistletoe plant has attached itself to the oak tree and is using the moisture and food from the tree to feed itself. Sometimes the mistletoe can get so large that it ends up killing its host. [5]

If you are here in the autumn, you will also see that the oak is losing its leaves. Most oak trees are **deciduous**, meaning they lose their leaves in the fall. You may not remember it, but you even had a deciduous part in your body. Baby teeth are also called deciduous teeth because they fall out as a part of the growing process. [10]

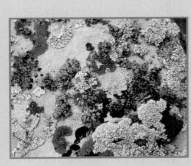

Stop 2 In contrast to the parasitic relationship of the mistletoe and the oak tree, here you see a **symbiotic** relationship in the **lichen** growing on the rocks at your feet. Lichen are plants made up of a fungus and an alga growing together. The fungi use the food made by the algae and the algae use the water absorbed by the fungi. The two materials help each other survive. Lichen grow on rocks and trees, and about sixteen thousand **species** have been identified. Some types of lichen are used as food by animals such as reindeer in the arctic areas and even by humans. Lichens are also used in making perfumes. As you continue your walk, look for the various colors of lichen from gray to green to white. When they are moist, the lichen are usually a bright green. [15] [20] [25]

Stop 3 The pine trees around you are examples of evergreens. Unlike deciduous trees, the leaves of evergreens stay green all year.

Stop 4 At the right time of year, you can enjoy the beauty of butterflies fluttering around you. Butterflies go through a four-stage **metamorphosis**. They go from egg to larva (a caterpillar) to pupa (the resting stage) to adult. The colorful butterflies you see are in the adult stage. Butterflies are useful to the woods as they often pollinate flowers. [30]

PREDICTING

For each set, write the definition on the line next to the word to which it belongs. If you are unsure, return to the reading on page 118, and underline any context clues you find. After you've made your predictions, check your answers against the Word List on page 123. Place a checkmark in the box next to each word whose definition you missed. These are the words you'll want to study closely.

SET ONE

a temporary stay	living off another species	animals	plants	innumerable

❑ 1. **flora** (line 2) _____

❑ 2. **fauna** (line 2) _____

❑ 3. **sojourn** (line 4) _____

❑ 4. **myriad** (line 4) _____

❑ 5. **parasitic** (line 5) _____

SET TWO

a change in form	shedding the leaves annually	organisms having common qualities
a beneficial relationship	an organism composed of a fungus and an alga	

❑ 6. **deciduous** (line 10) _____

❑ 7. **symbiotic** (line 16) _____

❑ 8. **lichen** (line 16) _____

❑ 9. **species** (line 21) _____

❑ 10. **metamorphosis** (line 31) _____

SELF-TESTS

1 Circle the word that best completes each sentence.

1. My (sojourn, myriad) in the Amazon only lasted five weeks, but I loved every minute of it.

2. After just three days of kindergarten, the child's (species, metamorphosis) from being extremely afraid to feeling confident was amazing.

3. The (fauna, flora) in the desert, from the brittle bush to the ocotillo plant, really bloom in the spring after a shower.

4. There were (parasitic, myriad) reasons why I was unable to make the meeting. I can't even start to tell you the problems I ran into that day.

5. The roommates' relationship became quite (symbiotic, parasitic) as they helped each other with homework and chores based on their strengths.

6. The (fauna, flora) in the woods include small animals such as squirrels and bigger animals like dear.

7. The (lichen, sojourn) covered the rocks and trees throughout the forest.

8. I think the autumn is a lovely time of year because the (parasitic, deciduous) trees in our neighborhood turn beautiful colors.

9. My friendship with Joanne started out well, but it has become (symbiotic, parasitic); all she does now is ask me for money and favors.

10. There are several (species, flora) of birds in the marsh, so we should have a great time bird watching this morning.

2 Finish the journal entries using the vocabulary words. Use each word once.

SET ONE

VOCABULARY LIST

| lichen | species | myriad | deciduous | flora |

October 29, 2006

My early morning hike in the forest was wonderful. The air was crisp, and wispy clouds blew across the sky. The (1)_____ trees are beginning to lose their leaves. Red, gold, and brown leaves carpeted the ground. The (2)_____ were a bright green in the morning mist. The (3)_____ had a magical quality: the flowers danced and the trees whispered to me. Every (4)_____ of plant seemed to have some advice, from the oak telling me to be strong to the dandelion urging me to go where the wind takes me. A (5)_____ of possibilities opened before me as I strolled through nature's majesty.

SET TWO

VOCABULARY LIST

| metamorphosis | fauna | sojourn | parasitic | symbiotic |

April 2, 2007

Today the first buds of spring are appearing on many of the trees. I am so lucky to be able to see the (6)_____ of the forest. I also spied a deer during my (7)_____. Of all the (8)_____ in the forest, the deer are my favorite. They are such beautiful creatures. I have always been afraid that my relationship with nature has been a (9)_____ one. I get so much

enjoyment from plants and animals, but have never felt that I have been able to give anything in return. Yesterday circumstances changed. I signed up to be a docent, and now the relationship can be (10) _____. I can still find peace from the forest, but I can also help to protect it by educating people about the joys of nature.

3 Match each item to the vocabulary word it best relates to. Use each word once.

VOCABULARY LIST

fauna	deciduous	lichen	flora	myriad
symbiotic	species	sojourn	parasitic	metamorphosis

1. pebbles on a beach, stars in the sky _____

2. ivy, roses _____

3. the homely girl in most teenage movies, moths _____

4. at the beach, to the mountains _____

5. maple trees, a stag's antlers _____

6. fox, squirrel _____

7. on rocks, on the sides of trees _____

8. the wood lily, the meadow lily _____

9. an unemployed relative who comes to stay and ends up watching television all day, fleas and ticks _____

10. the hermit crab and sea anemone, the white cattle egret and the elephant _____

WORD WISE

Word Pairs

Flora/Fauna: Flora (Chapter 19) means "the plants of a given region or period taken as a whole." Fauna (Chapter 19) means "the animals of a given region or period taken as a whole." The flora in my neighborhood park mainly consists of roses and geraniums, and the most abundant fauna are squirrels and pigeons.

Parasitic/Symbiotic: Parasitic (Chapter 19) means "pertaining to a parasite, such as a person who takes advantage of others." On the other hand, symbiotic (Chapter 19) means "any mutually beneficial relationship." My last romance involved a parasitic relationship—all my girlfriend cared about was my money. I am now looking for a symbiotic relationship where we can share interests and emotions.

Where Did It Come From?

Parasite (Chapter 19): comes from the Greek *para* "beside" and *sitos* "grain or food." Together *parasitos* originally meant "fellow guest." It came, however, to mean, even in ancient Greece, a professional dinner guest or "a person who takes advantage of others," such as eating often at someone's house and not returning the favor.

Your biology class has just taken the walk through Small Woods. Your instructor has given you the following worksheet to complete.

Name _____

1. List two types of fauna and two types of flora that you saw.

   _____ _____, _____ _____

2. Did you see any deciduous trees? How could you tell?

   _____

3. What color lichen did you see? Where did you spot the lichen?

   _____ _____

4. Name two species you saw.

   _____ _____

5. What stage of metamorphosis were the butterflies in?

   _____

6. Describe how humans have had a parasitic relationship with nature. What can we do to make our relationship with nature more symbiotic?

   _____

   _____

7. Although we do not have a myriad of choices of places for field trips, where do you suggest our next sojourn take us?

   _____

HINT

Mistakes as Learning Experiences

Making mistakes is part of the learning process. When you learned to ride a bike, you probably fell over a few times before you learned to keep your balance. The same idea applies to learning vocabulary. When you take a test, you may not get a perfect score. Look at the mistakes you made. Try to decide what went wrong. Did you read the question too fast? Did you misunderstand the question? Did you not study enough? Don't be so disappointed in a bad grade that you can't learn from the experience. You will do better next time if you take the time to understand what you did wrong this time. Also ask your instructor if you are unsure about why you got a question wrong; he or she wants to help you do better next time.

WORD LIST

deciduous
[di sij′ ōō əs]

adj. 1. shedding the leaves annually, as certain trees do
2. falling off at a particular stage of growth; transitory

fauna
[fô′ nə]

n. the animals of a given region or period taken as a whole

flora
[flôr′ ə, flōr′ ə]

n. the plants of a given region or period taken as a whole

lichen
[lī′ kən]

n. a complex organism composed of a fungus in symbiotic union with an alga, commonly forming patches on rocks and trees

metamorphosis
[met′ ə môr′ fə sis]

n. 1. a change in form from one stage to the next in the life of an organism
2. a transformation

myriad
[mir′ ē ad]

adj. of an indefinitely great number; innumerable
n. an immense number

parasitic
[par′ ə sit′ ik]

adj. pertaining to a parasite (1. an organism that lives on another species without aiding the host; 2. a person who takes advantage of others)

sojourn
[n. sō′ jûrn]
[v. sō jûrn′]

n. a temporary stay
v. to stay temporarily

species
[spē′ shēz, -sēz]

n. organisms having some common qualities; kind or type

symbiotic
[sim bē ot′ ik]

adj. 1. pertaining to symbiosis—the living together of two dissimilar organisms
2. any mutually beneficial relationship

WORDS TO WATCH

Which words would you like to practice with a bit more? Pick 3–5 words to study and list them below. Write the word, its definition, and compose your own sentence using the word correctly. This extra practice could be the final touch to learning a word.

	Word	Definition	Your Sentence
1.			
2.			
3.			
4.			
5.			

20 Review

Focus on Chapters 11–19

The following activities give you a chance to interact some more with the vocabulary words you've been learning. By looking at art, taking tests, answering questions, doing a crossword puzzle, and working with others, you will see which words you know well and which you still need to work with.

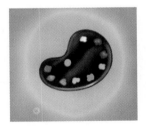

1. _____

2. _____

3. _____

4. _____

5. _____

6. _____

7. _____

8. _____

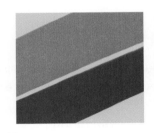

9. _____

10. _____

11. _____

12. _____

Match each picture on page 124 to one of the following vocabulary words. Use each word once.

VOCABULARY LIST

alfresco	visualization	plateau	personification	palette	lichen
multitude	affluence	enclave	portfolio	hues	peninsula

SELF-TESTS

1A Pick the word that best completes each sentence.

1. I need to make an appointment for my _____ checkup with the dentist.

   a. profuse   b. biannual   c. potent   d. derogatory

2. The _____ that best fits the atmosphere of my math class is that it's like being in a grave.

   a. simile   b. nada   c. enclave   d. plateau

3. The speaker's _____ gave me a chance to see whether I had written down all the major points he had made.

   a. zeitgeist   b. monopoly   c. escapade   d. summation

4. The _____ of my hometown on the news wasn't very flattering; I never thought of it as being filled with trash and crime.

   a. nomad   b. portfolio   c. depiction   d. testimony

5. On our last trip we discovered that several countries _____ an airport departure tax.

   a. levy   b. procure   c. wane   d. venerate

6. Because my grandmother is saving her doll collection for _____, I wasn't allowed to play with the dolls when I was little.

   a. imagery   b. posterity   c. summation   d. essence

7. Karl amused his dinner companions with a _____ about the waiter's service.

   a. motif   b. spectrum   c. fauna   d. bon mot

1B Complete the following sentences using the vocabulary words. Use each word once.

a. du jour	b. relevant	c. symbiotic	d. emblematic	e. flora

1. Sometimes it can be hard to find material that is _____ to one's argument, but for a good paper the writer must keep searching.

2. In biology we learned about _____ relationships among animals; I was amazed at the different ways species help each other.

3. The argument at the luncheon was _____ of all the problems the department is experiencing without strong leadership.

4. When my friend came to dinner, I wondered what the crisis _____ would be; she was never without a problem.

5. During the spring the _____ in the park is especially beautiful.

2 Finish the story using the vocabulary words. Use each word once.

VOCABULARY LIST

| ambiguous | equity | essence | expedition | faux pas | fortitude | inference |
| myriad | pristine | procure | ramifications | resolute | successive | volatile | wane |

THE VACATION THAT NEVER HAPPENED

My simple vacation became an adventure I would like to forget. Our plan was to go camping in the mountains, about five hours away. For a (1)_____ of reasons, we never quite made it. I thought my friend and I had agreed to take Friday off to avoid the weekend traffic. However, when I got to his house, he wasn't there. The obvious (2)_____ was that he had gone to work, so I called, and there he was. I asked him what had happened, but his reply was (3)_____. He never made it quite clear what had happened. I told him to forget it and just get to my house. Then we had to make (4)_____ stops to get items I thought Tom would have already had. He still had to (5)_____ his part of the groceries, reclaim his sleeping bag from the dry cleaners, and buy a book to read. My enthusiasm for this trip was starting to (6)_____. But I decided to remain (7)_____: this trip was going to happen.

Finally, we left town, but the (8)_____ of these delays became apparent as we hit the freeway. We ended up sitting in traffic for over an hour. After being in the driver's seat for four hours, I was ready for Tom to take over. However, he said he didn't feel like driving. I didn't think I was being unreasonable. All I was asking for was some (9)_____. The situation was starting to get (10)_____, but luckily we saw a sign that said the campground was close and we both calmed down. The (11)_____ woods and rivers called out to me. Their unspoiled beauty would relax me. I was thinking this (12)_____ might not turn out so bad after all. I was wrong.

At last we made it to the campground, and that was when I needed all my (13)_____ to keep from breaking down or killing Tom. He hadn't made the reservations, and there was no room for us.

Then Tom said it was my (14)_____ for trusting him to make the reservations. At that point, I was ready to throw Tom in the river, but I resisted. The (15)_____ of our friendship remains intact because basically Tom is a fun guy, but I'll think hard before I take another vacation with him.

▮▮▮▮ INTERACTIVE EXERCISE

Answer the following questions to further test your understanding of the vocabulary words.

1. What have you done that could be considered a magnanimous action?

   _____

2. If someone was making derogatory statements about a good friend of yours, what would you say to the person?

   _____

3. Write an anecdote about a friend or family member.

   _____

   _____

4. How can someone overcome metrophobia?

   _____

   _____

5. Name two ways a monopoly might be broken.

   _____

   _____

6. What kind of terrain do you enjoy walking on? _____

7. Where would you like to sojourn during the summer?

   _____

8. What is the foremost problem at your college? What is a possible solution?

   _____

   _____

9. What could change a person's perspective about a topic?

   _____

10. Give two examples of *la dolce vita.*

    _____

    _____

11. Name two types of fauna that you like.

    _____

    _____

12. In the spectrum of team sports, what two are your favorites to watch or play?

    _____

    _____

CROSSWORD PUZZLE

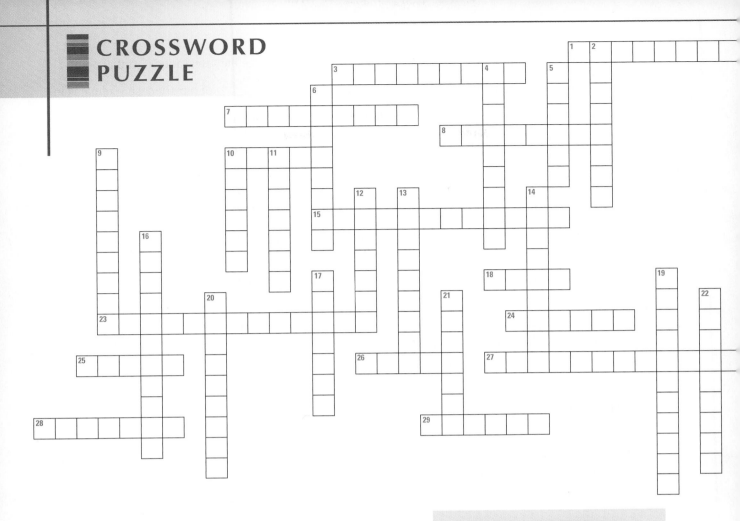

Across

1. suggestive
3. not rehearsed
7. pertaining to an organism that lives on another species without aiding the host
8. The moon is a crystal ball.
10. There it is!
15. a ghostly double
18. nothing
23. a change in form
24. powerful
25. a wanderer
26. the dominant theme
27. occurring after death
28. to grow
29. lightness of speech or manner

9. seize the day
10. the quality of being real
11. mental pictures
12. a kind or type
13. the spirit of the time
14. with trees, note this quality in autumn
16. an irregular variation
17. severe or stern
19. charming; vivid
20. a close friend
21. extravagant
22. weatlh; an abundance

Down

2. to regard with respect
4. evidence in support of a fact
5. to escape
6. an adventure

Use the following words to complete the crossword puzzle. You will use each word once.

VOCABULARY LIST

affluence	austere
burgeon	carpe diem
confidant	deciduous
doppelgänger	escapade
eschew	evocative
fluctuation	imagery
impromptu	levity
metamorphosis	metaphor
motif	nada
nomad	parasitic
picturesque	posthumously
potent	profuse
species	testimony
venerate	verity
voilà	zeitgeist

HINT

Read Carefully

When taking a test remember to read each question carefully. Sometimes students get a question wrong just because they read it too fast. Look for important words in a question such as "the least" or "always." If the test is multiple-choice, read each of the choices before making your decision. Be aware of choices such as "all of the above" or "none of the above" before you pick an answer. If it is a fill-in-the-blank test and you have several choices, try putting each choice in the blank and see which sounds best. Keep track of time limits, but don't stress over them. If you have studied enough, you will have time to read each question carefully and be able to finish the test.

▐▐▌▌▌ MIX IT UP

CATEGORY RACE

Get together with a dozen classmates or so and form three to four teams. Each team needs a set of flash cards for the words to be studied and a blank sheet of paper. Each team thinks of a category, writes it at the top of the piece of paper, and places flash cards that fit in that category underneath the heading. (Alternatively, you can write the words on the paper.) After ten minutes, call time. Each group reads its category and words. There may be some disagreement on whether a word fits the category; let consensus decide these issues. The team that uses the most words wins. Another way to play is to give each team the same category and seven minutes to record their words. You can also do this activity with each person making his or her own category list.

Possible categories:
1. travel words
2. words that show trouble
3. health-related words
4. history words
5. love-life words
6. crime-related words
7. business-related words
8. undesirable qualities

Sample sheet

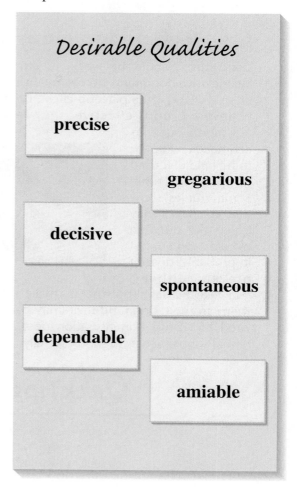

21 Medicine

A Healthy Dose of News

Health Watch

Your source for health and lifestyle tips

Do Herbal Medicines Work?

Consumers should be **wary**, as studies are still inconclusive for many herbal medicines. What is often working is the **placebo** effect. Because people believe a drug is effective, they feel better. A few herbs such as echinacea appear to be helpful if used for a short time. Some studies show that echinacea may lessen the duration of colds and flu, but it probably doesn't prevent either. If

you take herbal supplements, make sure you get them from a **bona fide** vitamin company. The Food and Drug Administration does not regulate herbal supplements, so shop carefully.

When to Worry About Forgetfulness

Dementia is a **dysfunction** that more people are becoming concerned about. Dementia is a deterioration in mental and social skills that is serious enough to have an influence on one's everyday activities. Dementia comes in several forms including Alzheimer's disease. You shouldn't be **paranoid** and think you are suffering from dementia if you forget where you put your car keys once or twice a month, but extreme forgetfulness can be a symptom. If you have any **qualms** about your or a loved one's mental health, talk to a physician to help determine whether the problem is serious or what may be causing the problem.

*Quick*Tips

Not every spot means cancer, and not every cancer is **malignant**. Some cancers can be cured. See your doctor about any unusual spots or moles or if you notice a change in a spot or mole.

Whenever you suspect a health problem, contact your doctor. With a proper examination, you can both decide whether the problem is **inconsequential**. If it bothers you, you should discuss the matter with your physician. If the problem is **perennial**, don't ignore it. Any enduring or recurring ailments should be examined.

5
10
15
20
25
30
35
40
45

▰▰▰ PREDICTING

For each set, write the definition on the line next to the word to which it belongs. If you are unsure, return to the reading on page 130, and underline any context clues you find. After you've made your predictions, check your answers against the Word List on page 135. Place a checkmark in the box next to each word whose definition you missed. These are the words you'll want to study closely.

SET ONE

genuine	disordered performance of a bodily system	cautious
a deterioration of intellectual abilities	a substance without medicine	

☐ 1. **wary** (line 4) _____

☐ 2. **placebo** (line 6) _____

☐ 3. **bona fide** (line 19) _____

☐ 4. **dementia** (line 25) _____

☐ 5. **dysfunction** (line 25) _____

SET TWO

threatening to life or health	everlasting	showing abnormal distrust
feelings of doubt	lacking importance	

☐ 6. **paranoid** (line 33) _____

☐ 7. **qualms** (line 38) _____

☐ 8. **malignant** (line 43) _____

☐ 9. **inconsequential** (line 47) _____

☐ 10. **perennial** (line 49) _____

▰▰▰ SELF-TESTS

1 Put a T for true or F for false next to each statement.

_____ 1. People should be wary of offers sent to their e-mail from companies or people they don't know.

_____ 2. A gas leak is an inconsequential problem.

_____ 3. Feeling paranoid makes it easy to cope with life.

_____ 4. Dealing with a teenager's desire for increased freedom has been a perennial problem for most parents.

_____ 5. When an airline announces a plane will be delayed due to "mechanical problems," most people would have qualms about later boarding the plane.

_____ 6. When a person is really ill, a dependable doctor will give the person a placebo.

_____ 7. Repeated trouble breathing could be a symptom of a dysfunction.

_____ 8. A man proposing to sell you his five-bedroom house on the beach in Malibu for $3,000 is probably making you a bona fide offer.

_____ 9. Some malignant tumors can be removed.

_____10. When a person cannot name every country in the world, he or she should be worried about dementia.

2 Use the vocabulary words to complete the following analogies. For instructions and practice, see Completing Analogies on page 6.

SET ONE

VOCABULARY LIST

| paranoid | malignant | wary | perennial | dementia |

1. a failing grade on a paper : disappointed :: a growling dog : _____
2. reading a good book : relaxing :: feeling that a killer lives on every block : _____
3. fleeting : _____ :: short : tall
4. cry : weep :: evil : _____
5. continually forgetting one's address : _____ :: laughter : happiness

SET TWO

VOCABULARY LIST

| dysfunction | bona fide | placebo | qualm | inconsequential |

6. dentist : drill :: hypochondriac : _____
7. a car seat : safe :: a diamond ring : _____
8. confidence : _____ :: cruelty : kindness
9. slipping on wet pavement : accident :: a bad kidney : _____
10. unimportant : _____ :: envy : jealousy

3 Complete the following sentences using the vocabulary words. Use each word once.

VOCABULARY LIST

| wary | dementia | dysfunction | placebo | bona fide |
| qualm | malignant | perennial | paranoid | inconsequential |

1. My friend is _____ that someone is listening to his phone conversations, so sometimes we have to speak in code.
2. Even though they are _____ losers, the town still supports the local baseball team because they are our team.

3. The historian wanted to make sure the manuscript was _____ before he began to use it for his paper on conditions during the Middle Ages.

4. My friend considered his comment about my bad cooking _____, but I took it seriously. I was really trying to improve my cooking skills.

5. My colleague has misplaced his office keys six times this month, forgotten where he parked eight times, and missed three important meetings due to forgetfulness. I am getting worried that he may be suffering from _____.

6. Four months after minor surgery my mother shouldn't be in pain, but she still wanted pills. At the family's request, the doctor began giving her a(n) _____ a month ago. My mother insists she feels better after taking them.

7. My major _____ about going camping this weekend is the weather. There is supposed to be a huge snowstorm in the mountains.

8. There was a(n) _____ in the baby's heart, so the doctor had to do an operation soon after birth.

9. I am _____ of ads for products that claim to be able to make me look twenty years younger or make me rich in one month.

10. We were so happy that my friend's tumor was not _____; she should be completely recovered in another year.

WORD WISE

Collocations

I made a *bona fide offer* on the car, but the owner didn't take me seriously. Because of the way I was dressed, he didn't think I could afford to buy it. (Chapter 21)

The river's flooding has become a *perennial problem* that the city can no longer afford to ignore now that the population is growing and people are moving closer to the riverbanks. (Chapter 21)

The pills the doctor gave Martha contained no medicine, so the lessening of her symptoms could be due to the *placebo effect.* (Chapter 21)

The *malignant tumor* continued to grow quickly, and the woman was dead within six months. (Chapter 21)

Word Pairs

Malignant/Benign: Malignant (Chapter 21) means "evil in nature." Benign means "showing gentleness or kindness." The woman's face looked benign, and we gladly welcomed her into our home unaware that there was a malignant purpose behind her visit.

Where Did It Come From?

Placebo (Chapter 21): comes from the Latin *placebo* "I shall please." The root is *placere* "to please." The word used with the meaning "a substance without medicine given to humor a patient" is first recorded in 1785.

Complete the following lists.

Times people should be wary

1. _____

2. _____

Items one would want to make sure are bona fide

1. _____ 2. _____

Signs of dementia

1. _____ 2. _____

Actions of a paranoid

1. _____

2. _____

Problems that are inconsequential

1. _____

2. _____

Body parts that often become dysfunctional

1. _____ 2. _____

Things that can be malignant

1. _____ 2. _____

Perennial problems in society

1. _____

2. _____

Qualms freshmen have about college

1. _____

2. _____

Times when a placebo might be given

1. _____

2. _____

HINT

A World of Words

Keep your eyes open for new words. You will certainly encounter new words in the textbooks you read in college and in the lectures your professors give, but new words can be found everywhere. Don't turn off your learning when you leave the classroom. When you see a new word in a newspaper or a newsletter or even on a poster downtown, use the strategies you have learned in this book: look for context clues around the new word, try to predict the meaning, and check the dictionary if you aren't sure of the meaning. No matter where you are or at what age you may be, your vocabulary can continue to grow.

bona fide [bō′ nə fīd′]	*adj.* 1. genuine 2. done or made in good faith; sincere
dementia [di men′ shə, -shē ə]	*n.* a deterioration of intellectual abilities along with emotional disturbances due to a brain disorder; madness
dysfunction [dis fungk′ shən]	*n.* disordered or impaired performance of a bodily system or organ
inconsequential [in kon′ sə kwen′ shəl]	*adj.* 1. lacking importance; petty 2. illogical; irrelevant *n.* a triviality
malignant [mə lig′ nənt]	*adj.* 1. threatening to life or health 2. evil in nature
paranoid [par′ ə noid′]	*adj.* showing unreasonable or abnormal distrust or suspicion *n.* one afflicted with paranoia
perennial [pə ren′ ē əl]	*adj.* 1. lasting through the year or through many years; everlasting 2. continually recurring
placebo [plə sē′ bō]	*n.* 1. a substance without medicine given to humor a patient 2. an inactive substance used as a control in an experiment 3. anything lacking real value done or given to humor another
qualm [kwäm, kwôm]	*n.* 1. a feeling of doubt or misgiving; uneasiness 2. a feeling of sickness, faintness, or nausea
wary [wâr′ ē]	*adj.* cautious; watchful

WORDS TO WATCH

Which words would you like to practice with a bit more? Pick 3–5 words to study and list them below. Write the word, its definition, and compose your own sentence using the word correctly. This extra practice could be the final touch to learning a word.

	Word	Definition	Your Sentence
1.			
2.			
3.			
4.			
5.			

22 Linguistics

The World of Words

Language evolves. New words enter a language, and old words become **archaic.** "Ye Olde Barber Shoppe" would be an appropriate name for a hair salon in an historic district, but if you used "ye" in common speech for "the," people wouldn't understand you, or they'd
5 find you a bit eccentric.

Some **neologisms** become part of a language, while others don't make it. In the last 150 years, people have tried to **coin** an **epicene,** or bisexual, pronoun. It can be awkward to always say "he or she" when speaking about a person of unknown gender. In the late 1800s Charles
10 Crozat Converse coined a blended word formed from "that one." For example, a sentence would read, "When a customer is angry, thon should be treated kindly." You wouldn't have to say, "He or she should be treated kindly." *Thon* was placed in a few dictionaries from 1898 to 1964 but never caught on with the speaking public. Today "they," "their," and "them" are being used more and more as both singular and plural pronouns. These
15 words have been used in the singular form for over one hundred years, but in some circles this use is still considered nonstandard and unacceptable.

Neologisms are formed in many ways. New words can be made by blending (such as *thon*), from people and place-names, and through abbreviations, among other methods. Blended words are also known as **portmanteau** words. Two common portmanteau words are *smog* from "smoke" and "fog"
20 and *brunch,* a combination of "breakfast" and "lunch." Words from proper names are called **eponyms.** *Braille* comes from Louis Braille, a French teacher of the blind. In the 1800s he invented a system of writing using raised dots to represent letters and other symbols that could be read by touch. The teddy bear was named after Teddy Roosevelt, president of the United States (1901–1909), in connection with his bear-hunting trips. Words that come from place-names are called **toponyms.** *Cashmere*
25 comes from Kashmir, India, where the Kashmir goat is found and whose fine wool is used in making yarn. *Cologne* is named after Cologne, Germany, where eau de cologne or cologne water has been made since 1709. Another way of creating neologisms is through abbreviation or **ellipsis.** For example, a *drawing room* once was called a *withdrawing room,* and over time the "with"
30 was omitted to give us a new word.

The field of **semantics** enriches our lives as we learn more about how languages are structured and how they change. Learning the **etymology** of a word can help a person remember the meaning of the word, as well as being a fascinating way to see how language changes. The history of words shows that language is dynamic, and we can't ex-
35 pect or shouldn't even want a language to remain static. As the world changes so will the ways we talk about it. Everyone should enjoy having thon's chance to explore the wonder of words.

▌▐▐ PREDICTING

For each set, write the definition on the line next to the word to which it belongs. If you are unsure, return to the reading on page 136, and underline any context clues you find. After you've made your predictions, check your answers against the Word List on page 141. Place a checkmark in the box next to each word whose definition you missed. These are the words you'll want to study closely.

SET ONE

| blending several features | to invent | new words | referring to either sex | a word rarely used today |

❏ 1. **archaic** (line 2) _____

❏ 2. **neologisms** (line 6) _____

❏ 3. **coin** (line 7) _____

❏ 4. **epicene** (line 7) _____

❏ 5. **portmanteau** (line 19) _____

SET TWO

| the shortening of a word | words based on a person's name | the history of a word |
| words derived from the name of a place | | a branch of linguistics that studies meaning |

❏ 6. **eponyms** (line 20) _____

❏ 7. **toponyms** (line 24) _____

❏ 8. **ellipsis** (line 28) _____

❏ 9. **semantics** (line 31) _____

❏ 10. **etymology** (line 33) _____

▌▐▐ SELF-TESTS

1 For each set, write the letter of the most logical analogy. See Completing Analogies on page 6 for instructions and practice.

SET ONE

_____ 1. sandwich : eponym ::   a. new inventions : neologisms

_____ 2. ancient : archaic ::   b. lengthening : ellipsis

_____ 3. rain : flowers grow ::   c. tennis : sport

_____ 4. hot : cold ::   d. look in a dictionary : etymology

_____ 5. phone rings : answer it ::   e. angry : mad

_____ 6. invent : coin ::

_____ 7. round : flat ::

_____ 8. semantics : linguistics ::

_____ 9. traveler : portmanteau ::

_____ 10. polka : a dance ::

f. Bermuda shorts : toponym

g. gardener : lawn mower

h. strong : epicene

i. microbiology : biology

j. couch : sofa

2 Match each example with the correct vocabulary word.

VOCABULARY LIST

semantics	toponym	portmanteau	coin	archaic
eponym	etymology	ellipsis	epicene	neologism

1. Ferris wheel (G. W. G. Ferris)

   _____

2. motel ("motor" + "hotel") _____

3. cab (cabriolet) _____

4. hamburger (Hamburg) _____

5. thou _____

6. addict: Latin *addictus* "assigned, surrendered"

   _____

7. screen saver _____

8. himorher _____

9. "Let's call it a patuka." _____

10. "I think the line means that he is foolish to be 'wasting' his time." "I think the line means that he is relaxing by 'wasting' his time." _____

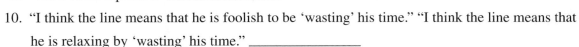

3 Complete each sentence using the vocabulary words. Use each word once.

VOCABULARY LIST

toponym	archaic	semantics	coin	portmanteau
ellipsis	neologism	epicene	eponym	etymology

1. Some of Juanita's habits are _____, such as wearing white gloves when she goes out, but she is a sweet old lady.

2. I was suspicious of the ad because of the _____ marks in it. I wondered what the original context was that had been shortened to "One reviewer calls it a '. . . great . . .' show."

3. A(n) _____ many people encounter every weekend is the food court.

4. I decided to check the _____ of the word *anger* before I wrote a definition paper in English. My instructor said that looking up the history of a word was a good step in trying to explain what it means.

5. It was interesting to find out that *tangerine* is a(n) _____ coming from Tangier, Morocco.

6. In science class we all had to invent something and then _____ a word for it.

7. It doesn't take much detective work to figure out that *platonic* is a(n) _____ derived from the philosopher Plato.

8. The art exhibit was a(n) _____ show with everything from paintings and sculptures to mobiles and pottery.

9. In my linguistics class, I found the area of _____ especially interesting; I enjoyed seeing how the meanings of words have changed through time.

10. I thought it was a(n) _____ excuse when Colin said he couldn't pick me up at the airport because his favorite team might be in the play-offs that night.

WORD WISE

Collocations

My uncle can easily *coin a phrase;* I am amazed at how quickly he can make up an expression. (Chapter 22)

Sometimes the *etymology of* a word can be surprising, which makes etymologies fun to read. (Chapter 22)

Where Did It Come From?

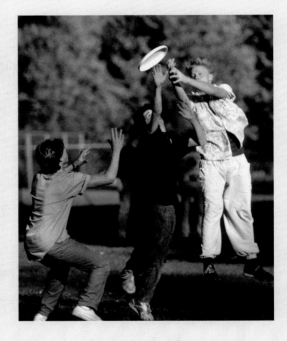

Eponym (Chapter 22): is formed from Greek *epi* "to" and *onoma* "name." An eponym is "a word based on a person's name." From the Charles Dickens novel *A Christmas Carol* we get the word *scrooge,* meaning a "stingy person" from the main character Ebenezer Scrooge. The Frisbee is named after William Frisbie who owned a pie company in Connecticut. In the late 1800s students at New England colleges played catch with his pie tins. *Mesmerize* comes from Frederich Mesmer, an Austrian physician who practiced hypnotism.

Portmanteau (Chapter 22): referring to blended words was coined by Lewis Carroll (1832–1898). A portmanteau is a kind of suitcase, and Carroll decided that two words put together, such as he used in his poem "Jabberwocky," had two meanings "packed up" in them. Among Carroll's portmanteau creations is *mimsy* from "miserable" and "flimsy" and *chortle,* which has become part of the English language, meaning "to laugh joyfully," from "chuckle" and "snort." Others have coined portmanteau words with one of the most common being *brunch,* a combination of "breakfast" and "lunch," originating around 1900. At one time the word *brunch* was so popular some scholars referred to blended words as "brunch words."

Answer the following questions about the vocabulary words.

1. If your name became an eponym, what would it refer to?

   _____

   _____

2. Coin a word and give the definition of the word.

   _____

   _____

3. Name two fields that have created several neologisms in the last decade.

   _____   _____

4. Come up with a toponym based on a place in your community. Explain why you picked this

   place. _____

   _____

5. What word do you think will become archaic in fifty years? Briefly explain your choice.

   _____

   _____

6. What would be your entry for an epicene pronoun?

   _____

7. Make up a portmanteau word and show what two words it comes from.

   _____

8. Look up the etymology of a word you find interesting and write the etymology here.

   _____

   _____

9. Use ellipsis to create a new word.

   _____

10. What word would it be easy to get into a semantic argument about?

    _____

HINT

Effective Studying

To make your study time profitable consider these points.

- Get a calendar or date book and write down the due dates for papers and other assignments and the dates for major tests. This initial preparation will let you carefully plan your study sessions.
- Gather everything you need to study and put it in your study area: books, pens, pencils, paper.
- Pay attention to what techniques work for you. After a test or assignment see whether taking notes, making outlines, or creating graphs or other drawings helped the most in remembering the topic.

archaic
[är kā′ ik]

adj. 1. of a word, often used in an earlier time but rarely used today
2. ancient, old-fashioned

coin
[koin]

v. 1. to invent; to fabricate
2. to make coins
n. a piece of metal money

ellipsis
[i lip′ sis]

n. 1. the shortening or abbreviation of a word
2. the omission from a sentence of a word or words that would make the sentence grammatically correct but aren't needed for clarity
3. a mark, such as . . . , to indicate an omission of letters or words

epicene
[ep′ i sēn′]

adj. 1. of a noun or pronoun, capable of referring to either sex
2. characteristic of both sexes
3. feeble, weak

eponym
[ep′ ə nim]

n. a word based on a person's name

etymology
[et′ ə mol′ ə jē]

n. the history of a word or part of a word

neologism
[nē ol′ ə jiz′ əm]

n. a new word or phrase or an existing word used in a new way

portmanteau
[pôrt man′ tō]

adj. combining or blending several features or qualities
n. a case or bag to carry clothing in while traveling

semantics
[si man′ tiks]

n. 1. a branch of linguistics dealing with the study of meaning, including the ways meaning changes over time
2. the meaning or an interpretation of the meaning of a word, sign, or sentence

toponym
[top′ ə nim′]

n. a word derived from the name of a place

WORDS TO WATCH

Which words would you like to practice with a bit more? Pick 3–4 words to study and list them below. Write the word, its definition, and compose your own sentence using the word correctly. This extra practice could be the final touch to learning a word.

	Word	Definition	Your Sentence
1.	_____	_____	_____
	_____		
2.	_____	_____	_____
	_____		
3.	_____	_____	_____
	_____		
4.	_____	_____	_____
	_____		

23 Political Science

Searching for the Ideal

Political systems have come in many forms over the course of human history. The quest for a **utopian** form of government has run the **gamut** from monarchies to democracies. Ancient Rome and the Soviet Union are two examples separated by time and
5 place that show the similarities and differences in how governments are run.

After the rule of a tyrannical king, the Romans formed a **republic** around 500 B.C. The senators of the republic worked together to make decisions regarding laws. This system worked
10 well until Rome began to expand and it became harder to control the many lands Rome had conquered. Eventually military power became more important than laws. In 62 B.C. Julius Caesar proposed a **triumvirate** with himself, the general Pompey, and the rich banker Crassus. These three men ruled Rome through
15 bribery, fear, and other methods. When the triumvirate collapsed, Pompey and Caesar went to war. Caesar won and became "Dictator for Life"; there was even talk of making Caesar a king. Rome had gone from a republic to a **totalitarian** government. Caesar did make improvements for the people such as fixing the
20 taxation system, making living conditions easier in the conquered territories, and changing the calendar. Still, his authoritarian rule was not appreciated, and seeing no other way to **oust** him, a group of nobles murdered Caesar in the Senate on the Ides of March (March 15) in 44 B.C.

Julius Caesar

25 In the 1800s the world was changing due to the rise of industrialism. The **milieu** was ripe for new ideas. Many people lived in slums and worked long hours in harsh conditions. Karl Marx was the voice for this class. In 1867 he published *Das Kapital,* explaining the class struggle between the poor and the rich. The
30 **proletariat** consisted of the workers who could gain power from the **bourgeoisie**, the property-owning capitalist class, only by

Karl Marx

revolution. Marx felt this revolution would take place in Germany or England where capitalism was well established, but it was Russia in 1917 that saw the start of communism. Lenin and Trotsky led the fight for workers' rights with Lenin becoming dictator of the newly named Union of Soviet
35 Socialist Republics (USSR). After Lenin's death in 1924, Stalin became dictator. Stalin began many reforms, but he also silenced all opposition. A totalitarian government was born again.

The USSR was dissolved in 1991, and the ideological **underpinnings** of communism have been shaken. Capitalism continues to thrive worldwide, although workers still fight for fair wages and safe working conditions. Humankind continues its search for an ideal form of government.

▌▌▌▌ PREDICTING

For each set, write the definition on the line next to the word to which it belongs. If you are unsure, return to the reading on page 142, and underline any context clues you find. After you've made your predictions, check your answers against the Word List on page 147. Place a checkmark in the box next to each word whose definition you missed. These are the words you'll want to study closely.

SET ONE

| the entire range | resembling an ideal place | a government with three people in power |
| a government that uses dictatorial control | | a state where power rests with the citizens |

❑ 1. **utopian** (line 2) _____

❑ 2. **gamut** (line 3) _____

❑ 3. **republic** (line 8) _____

❑ 4. **triumvirate** (line 13) _____

❑ 5. **totalitarian** (line 18) _____

SET TWO

| environment | a foundation | the working class | to remove | the property-owning class |

❑ 6. **oust** (line 22) _____

❑ 7. **milieu** (line 26) _____

❑ 8. **proletariat** (line 30) _____

❑ 9. **bourgeoisie** (line 31) _____

❑ 10. **underpinnings** (line 38) _____

▌▌▌▌ SELF-TESTS

1 Circle the correct meaning of each vocabulary word.

1. utopian: idealized   realized

2. republic: power with a dictator   power with the people

3. bourgeoisie: middle class   working class

4. triumvirate: rule by one   rule by three

5. oust: to remove   to add

6. gamut: range   one and only

7. milieu: emptiness   surroundings

8. proletariat: working class   middle class

9. totalitarian: liberal   authoritarian

10. underpinnings: basis   conclusion

2 Answer each question by writing the vocabulary word on the line next to the example it best fits. Use each word once.

SET ONE

VOCABULARY LIST

oust   triumvirate   utopian   gamut   totalitarian

1. Reginald told his bike racing team that he would order all the team's clothing in the sizes he thought people needed, and he would decide which races people would go to. What kind of leader is he? _____

2. The team decided to remove Reginald as their manager. What did they decide to do with him? _____

3. Reginald cried and then laughed when the team told him he had to go. What can be said about his emotions? _____

4. Reginald then joined with Karl and Miguel to be the leaders of a new team. What did the three of them form? _____

5. The three men feel that they will never argue with each other and that their team will win every race. What is their outlook on life? _____

SET TWO

VOCABULARY LIST

bourgeoisie   republic   proletariat   milieu   underpinnings

6. Keri just bought a house by the lake. What group has she become a part of according to Marxist theory? _____

7. Matthew rents an apartment and works as a busboy. What group does he belong to following Marxist theory? _____

8. Keri and Matthew get to vote for the president of their country. What kind of political system does their country have? _____

9. Matthew and Keri became friends when they met in the park at a soccer game. An avid interest in sports has cemented their friendship. What is a term for the basis of a relationship? _____

10. They both work in busy places: Keri in an office and Matthew at a restaurant. What is one's environment called? _____

3 Complete the reading using each word once.

THE SURVEY

For my political science class I took a survey asking students what life would be like in their

(1) _____ society. I was surprised at some of the responses I got. The answers ran the

(2) _____ from governments that gave citizens complete freedom to those that had strict

control of a person's every move. I was surprised at first by the woman who favored a(n)

(3) _____ form of government, but the more I talked to her, the more I saw that she didn't

like making any kind of decision. The (4) _____ of most people's societies were freedom

and equality. Most of the students favored a(n) (5) _____ and liked the idea of citizens get-

ting to make decisions about laws. Most people didn't want a class society. Several students said they

thought it was unfair how the (6) _____ had manipulated workers for years. A few people

even felt that in an ideal society, everyone would belong to the (7) _____ and work together

for the good of society, although several noted that this system hadn't been historically successful.

Most people felt the (8) _____ in the perfect society would be one of peace. One man wrote

on his survey, "I'd (9) _____ any whiners from my town, and then life would be great." For

fun, I asked my classmates what three people, dead or alive, they would pick if the government was

run as a(n) (10) _____. My favorite response was Oprah, Superman, and Princess Diana. The

survey helped me write an excellent paper on people's views of society and government.

WORD WISE

Collaborative Activity: Making a Scene

Creating scenes is a great activity if you enjoy acting or movement. Get together with six to nine classmates and divide into two to three groups. Each group creates a situation or uses one of the ideas below to write a short scene using at least five of the vocabulary words to be studied. Each group acts out the scene with the rest noting how the words are used. Discuss how the words fit in after the scene is completed. The scenes can also be done as role-playing with pairs creating the scenes instead of small groups. You can refer to the readings for ideas for your scenes. For example, referring to Chapter 21 one person could be a doctor and the other person a patient discussing a medical problem.

Scene possibilities: an audience at a concert for Chapter 2 or the theater for Chapter 9, people in an art gallery for Chapter 17, a class walking in the woods for Chapter 19, anthropologists investigating ruins for Chapter 26, travelers at Uluru or the Grand Canyon for Chapter 27, and customers at a store for Chapter 28.

Give two examples for each of the following situations.

EXAMPLE: milieu at a sporting event   *fans cheering* _____   *a scoreboard flashing* _____

1. **milieu** at a party   _____   _____

2. **proletariat** actions   _____   _____

3. **underpinnings** of a charity   _____   _____

4. characteristics of a **utopian** society _____   _____

5. circumstances that would cause a
   company to **oust** its president   _____   _____

6. actions of a **totalitarian** government _____   _____

7. a **gamut** of emotions   _____   _____

8. **bourgeoisie** behavior   _____   _____

9. actions in a **republic**   _____   _____

10. where a **triumvirate** could be found _____   _____

HINT

Banned Books

Freedom of expression has not always been a right granted to all people in all places. Over the centuries several books have been banned because of their content or wording. Many of the books that are now considered classics were banned at one time. A person doesn't have to like every book that is printed, but keeping an open mind about what one is asked to read in college or what one chooses to read later in life helps to foster creativity, critical thinking, and understanding in an individual.

The following are a few books that have been banned previously (Are any a surprise to you?):

Of Mice and Men by John Steinbeck   *The Color Purple* by Alice Walker
The Catcher in the Rye by J. D. Salinger   *James and the Giant Peach* by Roald Dahl
The House of Spirits by Isabel Allende   *To Kill a Mockingbird* by Harper Lee
Beloved by Toni Morrison   *Bless Me Ultima* by Rudolfo Anaya
Lord of the Flies by William Golding   *Harry Potter* (the series) by J. K. Rowling

WORD LIST

bourgeoisie
[boor′ zhwä zē′]

n. 1. in Marxist theory, the property-owning capitalist class
2. the middle class

gamut
[gam′ ət]

n. the entire scale or range

milieu
[mil yoo′]

n. environment; surroundings

oust
[oust]

v. to remove; to force out

proletariat
[prō′ li târ′ ē ət]

n. 1. in Marxist theory, the workers who do not own property and who must sell their labor to survive
2. the lowest or poorest class

republic
[ri pub′ lik]

n. 1. a state where power rests with the citizens
2. a state where the head of government is usually an elected president

totalitarian
[tō tal′ i târ′ ē ən]

adj. 1. pertaining to a government that uses dictatorial control and forbids opposition
2. authoritarian
n. an adherent of totalitarian principles or government

triumvirate
[trī um′ vər it, -və rāt′]

n. 1. a government of three rulers or officials functioning jointly
2. any group of three

underpinning
[un′ dər pin′ ing]

n. 1. a foundation or basis (often used in the plural)
2. material used to support a structure

utopian
[yoo tō′ pē ən]

adj. 1. resembling utopia, an ideal place
2. involving idealized perfection
3. given to impractical schemes of perfection

WORDS TO WATCH

Which words would you like to practice with a bit more? Pick 3–4 words to study and list them below. Write the word, its definition, and compose your own sentence using the word correctly. This extra practice could be the final touch to learning a word.

Word	Definition	Your Sentence
1.		
2.		
3.		
4.		

CHAPTER 24

Education

What's Your Personality?

It is obvious that people react differently in the same
situations and that people have job and hobby
preferences. In an effort to understand the reasons for
these differences, researchers began to **classify** people's
5 behaviors into different categories called personality
types. Katherine Briggs and her daughter Isabel Briggs-
Myers, beginning in the 1920s, developed one of the
most famous personality tests. They based their studies
on the Swiss psychologist Carl Jung's (1875–1961)
10 work. Jung felt people had **inherent** preferences and
that to lead a successful life one needed to focus on
those preferences and not try to change them. Briggs and her daughter took Jung's ideas and began to
study thousands of people to come up with questions that could lead to personality profiles. By 1956
they had developed a test that the Educational Testing Service (ETS), the group that administers the
15 Scholastic Aptitude Test (SAT), was willing to publish. There was some initial resistance to the test
since neither woman was a psychologist, but their work prevailed, and since then the Myers-Briggs
Type Indicator (MBTI) has been given to millions of people.

One area most personality tests examine is how people prefer to interact with others. The
questions aim to see whether a person is an **introvert** or **extrovert.** Introverts tend to be shy, and they
20 do not **relish** dealing with people. They prefer having a few friends to spend time with and they like
working alone. Extroverts, on the other hand, love meeting people, having lots of friends, and
working with others. In school, introverts and extroverts often look at being involved in group
projects differently, with extroverts usually welcoming working with others.

Another area of difference is how people perceive the world. Some people are known as
25 "sensors." They like to get information in a **sequential** order, they like facts, and they like hands-on
activities. These are the people who prefer to use their five senses to gather information. They are the
tactile people who want to touch something to test its reality. The other group is called "**intuitive.**"
They are fine with getting information in random order, and
they enjoy dealing with **abstract** ideas. In educational
30 settings these differences can lead to problems. Most
elementary school teachers, about 70%, are sensory types
and most people are sensory types, also about 70%. The
predominance of sensory early-learning teachers works well
for most young students, but about 77% of college professors
are the intuitive type. For many sensors, a college lecture
35 given by an intuitive, who freely makes random observations
and uses generalities, becomes frustrating. They want an
outline; they want order. They want concrete examples. This
difference makes getting a college education difficult for
some personality types.

40   Another difference is whether people are "thinkers" or "feelers" when they make decisions. Thinkers are very logical. They tend to be detached and their goal is fairness. Feelers are more concerned with how the results of a decision will impact other people. They are concerned with harmony over justice. The last type of difference features the "judgers" and the "perceivers." Judgers like an orderly environment. They make a plan and stick to it. Perceivers prefer to be spontaneous. They don't like to make firm decisions. For this type what works one day might not be the right thing to do the next day.

45   The MBTI asks questions that help people create a personality profile that includes the four ways of interacting with the world. Two possible personality types are the ISTJ (Introvert, Sensor, Thinker, Judger) and the ENFP (Extrovert, Intuitive, Feeler, Perceiver). These two types deal with situations differently, and they relate to each other differently, which can sometimes lead to arguments and stressful situations. It can be helpful to understand these differences to better get along with each

50   other and to better know oneself. Personality profiles don't try to confine the individual. They allow for the **multifaceted** nature of each person, but they can help a person see one's preferences. An awareness of why one behaves a certain way can assist a person in a variety of life's activities from education and career choices to romance and money management.

▌▌▌▌ PREDICTING

For each set, write the definition on the line next to the word to which it belongs. If you are unsure, return to the reading on page 148, and underline any context clues you find. After you've made your predictions, check your answers against the Word List on page 153. Place a checkmark in the box next to each word whose definition you missed. These are the words you'll want to study closely.

SET ONE

| innate | to enjoy | to organize | an outgoing person | a shy person |

❏ 1. **classify** (line 4) _____

❏ 2. **inherent** (line 10) _____

❏ 3. **introvert** (line 19) _____

❏ 4. **extrovert** (line 19) _____

❏ 5. **relish** (line 20) _____

SET TWO

| pertaining to the sense of touch | an idea not related to a specific example |
| many-sided | in order | instinctive |

❏ 6. **sequential** (line 25) _____

❏ 7. **tactile** (line 27) _____

❏ 8. **intuitive** (line 27) _____

❏ 9. **abstract** (line 29) _____

❏ 10. **multifaceted** (line 51) _____

1 Match each term with its synonym in Set One and its antonym in Set Two.

SYNONYMS

ANTONYMS

SET ONE

SET TWO

_____ 1. intuitive   a. concrete

_____ 2. classify   b. innate

_____ 3. tactile   c. sensitive

_____ 4. relish   d. enjoy

_____ 5. inherent   e. sort

_____ 6. abstract   f. simple

_____ 7. extrovert   g. extrovert

_____ 8. multifaceted   h. concrete

_____ 9. sequential   i. random

_____ 10. introvert   j. introvert

2 Finish the following fictitious headlines. Use each word once.

1. Extreme _____ Emerges After Three Years in House Alone

2. Mayor Declares She Will _____ Rejuvenating Decaying Downtown Shopping Area

3. *Study Suggests Kindness _____ in All People*

4. Professor's _____ Ideas on Time Travel Win Science Foundation Award

5. _____ Invites 100 People to Party in Small Apartment: Trouble Erupts

6. Project to _____ Local Bird Species Continues

7. *New _____ Display at Children's Museum Lets Kids Feel River and Ocean Elements*

8. City Council Advocates _____ Plan to Restructure City Departments

9. _____ *Actor Impresses Audiences with Singing and Dancing Skills*

10. Musician Credits _____ Powers for His Productive Song Writing Career

VOCABULARY LIST

introvert	relish
inherent	abstract
extrovert	classify
tactile	sequential
multifaceted	intuitive

3 For each set, complete the analogies. See Completing Analogies on page 6 for instructions and practice.

SET ONE

1. faulty : flawed :: innate : _____
2. impossible : likely :: extrovert : _____
3. photographer : shoot :: librarian : _____
4. losing : disappointment :: _____ : insights
5. comedy : laugh :: dessert : _____

SET TWO

6. sunset : visual :: a shower : _____
7. farewell : good-bye :: _____ : outgoing
8. cow : animal :: economic problems : _____
9. yell : whisper :: _____ : random
10. barber : cut :: dentist : _____

WORD WISE

Collocations

The game brought out a *gamut of emotions* from sadness and anger to eventual happiness. (Chapter 23)

Putting a process in *sequential order* makes it easier to understand how to do it. (Chapter 24)

Word Pairs

Bourgeoisie/Proletariat: Bourgeoisie (Chapter 23) in Marxist theory means "the property-owning capitalist class." Proletariat (Chapter 23), also in Marxist theory, refers to "the workers who do not own property and who must sell their labor to survive." On a Saturday afternoon, the bourgeoisie enjoy a relaxing stroll through the park, while the proletariat continue to toil in the factories.

Connotations and Denotations

Introvert and Extrovert (Chapter 24): denotation of introvert—"a shy person" and of extrovert—"an outgoing person." Depending on your personality type and experiences your connotation of an introvert might be a quiet person with deep thoughts or a bore. You may see an extrovert as fun and friendly or loud and obnoxious. Picture a person for each type. What is the person doing? Did you picture someone you know? These visualizations may help you understand your connotations for each type.

Where Did It Come From?

Utopian (Chapter 23): the noun Utopia comes from Greek *ou* "not" plus *topos* "a place," and means "nowhere." The word was coined by Thomas More in 1516 to use as the title of his book about an imaginary ideal island society. A utopia (lower case) is "any ideal place" and the adjective utopian means "resembling utopia."

For each word give an example of how it could apply to a situation in college.

EXAMPLES:

tactile   carrying ten books home from the library

inherent   joining the school chorus to use the excellent voice one was born with

1. tactile   _____

2. abstract   _____

3. classify   _____

4. inherent   _____

5. extrovert   _____

6. introvert   _____

7. sequential   _____

8. intuitive   _____

9. multifaceted   _____

10. relish   _____

HINT

Journal Writing

Keeping a journal can improve your writing, reading, and critical thinking skills. You can also build your vocabulary by using some of the new words you are learning in your entries. When you take the time to write about your feelings and observations of the world, it allows you to reflect on what is happening in your life and often better deal with problems you encounter. You don't have to write in the journal every day; even writing a few times a week will help develop your skills. The following are a few ideas for your journal: describe the people and experiences that you encounter, look at changes in your life, examine your goals for the future, explore your reactions to a movie you have seen or something you have read (a short story, a newspaper article, a textbook chapter), record your experiences with music, food, sports, travel, or a hobby. There is really no end to the ideas that can be captured in a journal. Don't strain to come up with something to write about; let the ideas flow naturally. Enjoy the writing and exploration process. Remember that the journal is for you, so don't worry about other people's reactions to what you write.

abstract
[adj. and v. ab strakt',
n. ab' strakt, ab' strakt]

adj. 1. an idea not related to a specific example
2. not easily understood; complex
v. 1. to take out; to extract
2. to summarize; to condense
n. a summary

classify
[klas' ə fī']

v. 1. to organize; to categorize; to sort
2. to limit information to approved people

extrovert
[ek' strə vûrt']

n. an outgoing person

inherent
[in hēr' ənt, -her']

adj. existing in someone or something as a permanent quality; innate

introvert
[in' trə vûrt']

n . a shy person

intuitive
[in tōō' i tiv]

adj. instinctive; perceptive; sensitive

multifaceted
[mul' tē fas' i tid, tī-]

adj. many-sided; versatile; complex

relish
[rel' ish]

v. 1. to enjoy; to take pleasure in
2. to like the taste of
n. pleasurable appreciation of anything; liking

sequential
[si kwen' shəl]

adj. characterized by a regular order of parts; in order; following

tactile
[tak' til, -tīl]

adj. pertaining or perceptible to the sense of touch; concrete

■■■■■ WORDS TO WATCH

Which words would you like to practice with a bit more? Pick 3–4 words to study and list them below. Write the word, its definition, and compose your own sentence using the word correctly. This extra practice could be the final touch to learning a word.

Word	Definition	Your Sentence
1. _____	_____	_____
_____	_____	_____
2. _____	_____	_____
_____	_____	_____
3. _____	_____	_____
_____	_____	_____
4. _____	_____	_____
_____	_____	_____

25 Word Parts III

Look for words with these **prefixes, roots,** and/or **suffixes** as you work through this book. You may have already seen some of them, and you will see others in later chapters. Learning basic word parts can help you figure out the meanings of unfamiliar words.

prefix: a word part added to the beginning of a word that changes the meaning of the root

root: a word's basic part with its essential meaning

suffix: a word part added to the end of a word; indicates the part of speech

WORD PART	MEANING	EXAMPLES AND DEFINITIONS
Prefixes		
meta-	change	*metamorphosis:* a change in form *metabolism:* the physical and chemical changes in an organism that make energy available
multi-	many, much	*multitude:* an indefinite number; many *multicolored:* many-colored
neo-	new, revived, modified	*neologism:* a new word or phrase *neoclassical:* pertaining to a revival of classical styles in art, literature, music, or architecture
para-	next to, almost, beyond, abnormal	*paraphrase:* a restatement of a passage *parallel:* going in the same direction; next to each other
Roots		
-annu-, -enni-	year	*biannual:* happening twice each year *perennial:* lasting through many years
-fid-	faith, trust	*bona fide:* done in good faith *confide:* to have trust
-mut-	change	*permutation:* the act of changing *mutant:* a new type of organism due to a change in a gene or chromosome
-sequ-	to follow	*inconsequential:* not worth following; lacking importance *sequel:* a literary work or film that follows the same story of a preceding work
-tract-	to drag, to pull, to draw	*abstract:* to draw or take away *tractor:* a vehicle used to pull things

Suffixes

-esque (makes an adjective)	resembling, relating to	*picturesque:* resembling a picture *Romanesque:* relating to Rome
-oid (makes an adjective)	like, resembling	*paranoid:* like or suffering from paranoia (an excessive distrust of others) *humanoid:* resembling humans
-ure (makes a verb)	action or process	*censure:* process of expressing disapproval *failure:* action of failing

▊▊▊▊ SELF-TESTS

1 Read each definition and choose the appropriate word. Use each word once. The meaning of the word part is underlined to help you make the connection. Refer to the Word Parts list if you need help.

1. star<u>like</u> _____

2. the <u>process</u> of coming into use _____

3. lasting 100 <u>years</u> _____

4. a <u>new</u>born child _____

5. a person trained to work <u>next to</u> a lawyer or teacher _____

6. to <u>draw</u> or take away _____

7. a person one puts <u>trust</u> in _____

8. <u>resembling</u> a picture _____

9. to <u>change</u> a penalty to a less severe form _____

10. the <u>following</u> of one thing after another _____

> **VOCABULARY LIST**
>
> | | |
> |---|---|
> | asteroid | commute |
> | inure | sequence |
> | neonate | centennial |
> | picturesque | abstract |
> | paraprofessional | confidant |

2 Finish the sentences with the meaning of each word part. Use each meaning once. The word part is underlined to help you make the connection.

VOCABULARY LIST

draw	many	revived	process	almost
year	resemble	change	follow	faith

1. Andr<u>oid</u>s are popular characters in science fiction movies because they _____ human beings; therefore, they are easy to costume.

2. The <u>mut</u>ant ant was able to carry twice as much as a normal ant. The _____ made it a valuable addition to the nest.

3. The book I just finished is a good example of <u>neo</u>romanticism. It _____ the romantic movement's interest in the importance of nature.

4. The <u>sequ</u>el continues to _____ Nita's adventures, but now she is three years older and entering college.

5. My paraphrase was _____ like the original quote, but I made sure to use enough of my own words and style to avoid stealing.

6. I was able to procure the special chocolates my husband likes, but the _____ wasn't easy. I had to call ten places to find where I could order them.

7. I am not worried about my girlfriend's fidelity; I have _____ in her loyalty.

8. My husband usually forgets our anniversary, but he remembered this _____.

9. The store was able to _____ me in with their attractive window display.

10. Because I work for a multinational corporation, I could be transferred to _____ countries.

3 Finish the story using the word parts. Use each word part once. Your knowledge of word parts, as well as the context clues, will help you create the correct words. If you do not understand the meaning of a word you have made, check the dictionary for the definition or to see whether the word exists.

WORD PARTS LIST

esque	sequ	neo	oid	annu
meta	fid	mut	tract	ure

THE RUN

It was time for the town's (1)_____al Mud Run, and this year I was going to participate for the first time. Being a (2)_____phyte, I wasn't sure what to expect. I hoped I could end(3)_____ the distance, the hills, and, most of all, the mud. I was a bit intimidated when I saw my statu(4)_____ competitors. They all looked like they had stepped off a pedestal at a Greek temple. Then I started to hear the animal (5)_____phors: "I'm a stampeding elephant," "I'm a leopard waiting to leap." I became an ostrich ready to put my head in the sand. But I got my con(6)_____ence back and took off with everyone else when the gun sounded. My progress was hindered at the first water crossing. I was paran (7)_____ about getting wet. Finally, I decided that I didn't want to pro(8)_____ the race, so I jumped in and got soaked. We did three laps, and every lap there was some (9)_____ation in the course. With all the runners going by, the conditions changed each lap. At last, I crossed the finish line in third place. I was overjoyed. I had not, however, anticipated the con(10)_____ence of doing the race. I have become an addict for mud runs, and have now competed in over fifty races.

4 Pick the best definition for each underlined word using your knowledge of word parts. Circle the word part in each of the underlined words.

a. relating to the writings of Franz Kafka

b. resembling the truth but unproven

c. always faithful

d. unchangeable

e. a person who changes a literary work from one form to another

f. beyond the usual

g. a comment that doesn't follow the preceding one

h. to draw away

i. happening every two years

j. a university with many campuses

_____ 1. The Internet has helped to spread several factoids; people read the same stories about killer bananas or ways to earn thousands of dollars and think the stories are real.

_____ 2. Curtis is studying paranormal activities such as clairvoyance and extrasensory perception.

_____ 3. Going to a multiversity can be tiring. I have to drive to four different campuses this semester to get to all my classes.

_____ 4. My life at work has become Kafkaesque since the new manager insists on changing procedures without telling anyone. I am never sure what is going on anymore.

_____ 5. The U.S. Marine Corps motto—*semper fidelis*—shows the dedication of marines to their duties.

_____ 6. Unfortunately, Verda was immutable about her vacation plans, and she went to the mountains to ski even though there wasn't any snow.

_____ 7. I found it hard to understand the speaker because his speech was filled with non sequiturs. His comments just didn't connect to one another.

_____ 8. The Olympics are a biennial celebration of athletics worldwide.

_____ 9. I put the rusted statue in the garage; now it won't detract from the appeal of the house.

_____ 10. My uncle is a metaphrast; he changes short stories into poems.

5 A good way to remember word parts is to pick one word that uses a word part and understand how that word part functions in the word. Then you can apply that meaning to other words that have the same word part. Use the words to help you match the word part to its meaning.

SET ONE

_____ 1. **multi-:** multitude, multiply, multifaceted

_____ 2. **meta-:** metamorphosis, metaphor, metabolism

_____ 3. **-fid-:** confide, fidelity, bona fide

_____ 4. **-sequ-:** sequential, sequel, consequence

_____ 5. **-oid:** humanoid, paranoid, android

a. to follow

b. change

c. many, much

d. faith, trust

e. resembling, like

SET TWO

_____ 6. **para-:** parallel, parasite, paranormal   f. new, revived, modified

_____ 7. **neo-:** neologism, neophyte, neoclassical   g. year

_____ 8. **-mut-:** permutation, commute, mutation   h. action or process

_____ 9. **-annu-, -enni-:** annual, anniversary, perennial   i. change

_____ 10. **-ure:** censure, endure, procedure   j. next to, almost, beyond, abnormal

WORD WISE

Internet Activity: For Further Reading and Research

When the readings in this text capture your attention you can turn to the Internet for more information. When you see a vocabulary word you have been studying on a Web site, note how it is used. You will also likely come across some new words where you can practice your context clue skills to discover a meaning. Here are a few sites to get you started in your quest for more information.

For more on immigration, Angkor Wat, Julius Caesar, Karl Marx, or the former Soviet Union try www.historychannel.com. At the History Channel's Web site you can type in the time period, person, or event you are interested in, and you'll have a choice of several articles to click on; see what interests you most.

To find out more about a variety of health-related issues in the United States and worldwide go to www.nih.gov/ for the National Institutes of Health or www.who.int/en/ for the World Health Organization.

To explore the art and entertainment world try www.salon.com for articles on a variety of creative interests from movies to music.

INTERACTIVE EXERCISE

Use the dictionary to find a word you don't know that uses each word part listed below. Write the meaning of the word part, the word, and the definition. If your dictionary has the etymology (history) of the word, see how the word part relates to the meaning, and write the etymology after the definition.

Word Part	Meaning	Word	Definition and Etymology
EXAMPLE: -sequ-	to follow	sequela	an abnormal condition resulting from a previous disease. From Latin sequela, what follows
1. -annu-			

2. *meta-* _____

_____

_____

3. *-mut-* _____

_____

_____

4. *neo-* _____

_____

_____

5. *-tract-* _____

_____

_____

HINT

Idioms

An idiom is a phrase where the meaning of the words cannot be taken literally; the meaning is something other than what the words would usually mean. For example, if you ask your friend what he will do if he misses his connecting flight and he says, "I'll cross that bridge when I come to it," you would not really expect to see him walk across a bridge at the airport. But the idiom does give a vivid picture of a person facing a situation or problem when it happens. Using context clues can often help you figure out the meaning of an idiom.

Students usually want to avoid using idioms in their college papers because they are an informal way of communicating. Idioms, however, are used in informal writing and in speech. They are especially used in speech because they can be a vivid way of speaking. Watch where you find idioms and how you use them yourself.

There are hundreds of idioms in use in English today, and new idioms are sometimes created. Other languages also have idioms that are often similar to ones in English. To find out more about idioms look for idiom dictionaries that give the meaning and, when known, the history of an idiom.

Can you figure out the meanings of the idioms (in bold) in the following sentences?

I **slept like a log** after getting home from an eight-hour hike.

After my mother got a promotion at work, we **painted the town red.**

I **made a beeline** for the dessert table when I saw my aunt's special pecan pie.

26 Anthropology

Societies and Customs

The Mayan culture continues to intrigue modern society. One of the great centers of Mayan culture was Chichen-Itza on the Yucatan Peninsula. Life at Chichen-Itza was hardly **immutable.** Roughly between 500 and
5 1400, a site of numerous temples, a huge ball court, and an astronomical observatory burgeoned in the tropical jungle. The Maya abandoned the site twice, and around 1200 the Toltecs from the north invaded the area, adding their religion and architecture to the Mayan concepts.
10 Anthropologists and archeologists have been **meticulous** in studying the ruins at Chichen-Itza to discover the customs of this ancient society.

The Castillo

     What made life **viable** for the Maya at Chichen-Itza were the *cenotes* or wells. The name *chichen* shows the
15 importance of the wells to the society. *Chi* meant "mouths" in Mayan and *chen* meant "wells." These wells provided a source of water for a community composed of a **hierarchy** of slaves, farmers, hunters, merchants, warriors, priests, and nobles. Each group had its special role to play to keep the community functioning. The cenotes also hold a clue to the religious
20 **rituals** of the Maya: several bodies have been found in the wells. Human sacrifice, though generally considered **heinous** by today's standards, was a part of Mayan religious practices. Other **artifacts** found in the cenotes include jewelry and dolls. The Maya had several gods, and the sacrifices of young women and objects may have been used to **quell** the wrath of a rain god or pay homage to the god of maize. Because the gods controlled the weather and therefore the food supply, it was essential for the
25 people to keep the gods happy. Bloodletting, especially of the ears and tongue, was another way a person could earn favor with a god.

     Religious beliefs were also **manifested** in the architecture and games of the Maya. An impressive and **ominous** area at Chichen-Itza is the Great Ball Court, the largest found at a Mayan site. The ballgame was played between two teams and seems to have
30 involved keeping a rubber ball from touching the ground without using the hands. The game was over when the ball went through a scoring ring attached to the walls of the court. The winner of the game did not receive the prize people today would expect. The captain of the winning team would offer his head to the leader of
35 the losing team for decapitation. It was part of the Mayan religious beliefs that dying quickly was a great honor, and they obviously felt that the winner of this contest deserved such an honor.

A chacmool figure introduced by the Toltecs, possibly used in heart sacrifices.

     The Maya were a highly advanced society, demonstrated in their complex temple designs, accurate calendar, and elaborate
40 artwork. The Maya continue to fascinate the world with their customs and achievements.

▎▊▍▎ PREDICTING

For each set, write the definition on the line next to the word to which it belongs. If you are unsure, return to the reading on page 160, and underline any context clues you find. After you've made your predictions, check your answers against the Word List on page 165. Place a checkmark in the box next to each word whose definition you missed. These are the words you'll want to study closely.

SET ONE

possible	set procedures for a ceremony	unchangeable
extremely careful	a system of persons ranked one above the other	

❑ 1. **immutable** (line 4) _____

❑ 2. **meticulous** (line 11) _____

❑ 3. **viable** (line 13) _____

❑ 4. **hierarchy** (line 18) _____

❑ 5. **rituals** (line 20) _____

SET TWO

any objects made by humans	revealed	evil	to quiet	threatening

❑ 6. **heinous** (line 21) _____

❑ 7. **artifacts** (line 21) _____

❑ 8. **quell** (line 23) _____

❑ 9. **manifested** (line 27) _____

❑ 10. **ominous** (line 28) _____

▎▊▍▎ SELF-TESTS

1 Match each term with its synonym in Set One and its antonym in Set Two.

SYNONYMS
SET ONE

_____ 1. heinous   a. workable

_____ 2. quell   b. object

_____ 3. meticulous   c. calm

_____ 4. artifact   d. vicious

_____ 5. viable   e. thorough

ANTONYMS
SET TWO

_____ 6. ritual   f. equality

_____ 7. immutable   g. hidden

_____ 8. hierarchy   h. variety

_____ 9. ominous   i. changeable

_____ 10. manifest   j. safe

2 Complete the sentences using the vocabulary words. Use each word once.

1. My mother's negative reaction was _____ about my little sister taking a trip to India with a man she met a month ago.

2. The museum displayed _____ from the Inca civilization including beautifully decorated pots.

3. Alicia was quick to _____ the rumor that she was engaged to Brian; she assured people they were just friends.

4. The _____ music signaled the entrance of the villain.

5. The people decided that the mountain was not a(n) _____ place to live after their crops failed two years in a row.

6. His love for Amanda was _____ to everyone but Carlos.

7. It was a(n) _____ action by the vandals to break all the windows in the auditorium the day before the graduation ceremony.

8. I was _____ in following the instructions for the cake, so I don't understand why it tasted horrible.

9. To get things done at my office, it is essential to understand the _____ from supervisor on down.

10. The _____ practices of different societies are interesting to study, especially marriage customs.

3 Complete the readings using each word once.

DAY 1

The plane is about to take off. I am so excited about my summer trip to the South Pacific to gather information on how the local people live. I am especially excited about seeing their (1)_____. I became intrigued about island customs after reading Margaret Mead's book *The Coming of Age in Samoa*. Her (2)_____ work in observing and recording the behaviors of the people fascinated me. I am also curious whether the (3)_____ system is still functioning the same or whether people can move between ranks more easily now. I wasn't sure that making a living as an anthropologist was a(n) (4)_____ idea, but when I started college two years ago, I decided to pursue a subject I love. I know that the society I am about to visit has not been (5)_____, but I hope to see some of the practices that my hero Mead saw.

VOCABULARY LIST

heinous	ominous	artifacts	quell	manifest

Today we visited some (6)_____: an army of ancient carved figures used to guard a sacred ceremonial site. The faces were (7)_____ with big red eyes and long tongues sticking out of huge mouths. If someone dared to walk past the statues, he or she was sure to anger the gods. The natives believed that (8)_____ troubles would befall a person who entered the taboo area. Because of the strong belief in a statue's power, illnesses could (9)_____ themselves in a person. It took herbal medicines and potent ceremonies to (10)_____ the fears and difficulties of those that disturbed the sacred place.

WORD WISE

Internet Activity: For Further Vocabulary Study

For a list of challenging words, several of which you are learning in this text, and how many times a word has appeared in the *New York Times* in the last year with an example of the word in context visit www.nytimes.com/learning/students/wordofday.

For dictionary entries, a word of the day feature, and word-related games give the Merriam-Webster Online dictionary at www.m-w.com a look.

For a list of more Web sites related to vocabulary study look on the back cover of this text. Enjoy exploring the Internet's many resources, but watch your time. It can be easy to lose track of time as you link from one site to the next.

Pretend you have the opportunity to interview an anthropologist. Write six questions you would ask the person using at least six of the vocabulary words. You don't need to know the answers to the questions. Pick one or more societies to ask about. For example: What is the most interesting artifact you have found in Egypt?

1. _____
   _____

2. _____
   _____

3. _____
   _____

4. _____
   _____

5. _____
   _____

6. _____
   _____

HINT

Marking Words When Reading

When you read for fun, it can be counterproductive to stop and look up every word you don't know—you will become frustrated with reading instead of enjoying it. As this book advocates, looking for context clues is the best way to find the meaning of an unknown word, but sometimes this method doesn't work. There are other ways of keeping track of unfamiliar words; try these methods to see which fits your style.

- Keep a piece of paper and a pen next to you and write down the word and page number.
- Keep a piece of paper next to you and rip it into small pieces or use sticky notes. Put a piece between the pages where the word you don't know is located. For added help, write the word on the paper.
- If the book belongs to you, circle the words you don't know and flip through the book later to find them.
- If the book belongs to you, dog-ear the page (turn the corner down) where the word you don't know is located. This method is useful when you don't have paper or a pen handy.
- Repeat the word and page number to yourself a few times. Try to connect the page number to a date to help you remember it.

When you are done reading for the day, get your dictionary and look up the words you marked. The last two methods work best if you don't read many pages before you look up the words or if there are only a few words you don't know. Using these methods will help you learn new words without destroying the fun of reading. Note: If you come across a word you don't know several times and not knowing its meaning hinders your understanding of what is going on, then it's a good idea to stop and look up the word.

WORD LIST

artifact
[är′ tə fakt′]

n. any object made by humans; a handmade object or the remains of one, such as found at an archeological dig

heinous
[hā′ nəs]

adj. wicked; vile; evil

hierarchy
[hi′ ə rär′ kē,
hi′ rär′ kē]

n. a system of persons or things ranked one above the other

immutable
[i myoo′ tə bəl]

adj. unchangeable

manifest
[man′ ə fest′]

v. to reveal; to show plainly
adj. obvious; evident
n. a list of cargo or passengers

meticulous
[mə tik′ yə ləs]

adj. 1. extremely careful and precise
2. excessively concerned with details

ominous
[om′ ə nəs]

adj. 1. threatening; menacing
2. pertaining to an evil omen

quell
[kwel]

v. 1. to quiet; to pacify
2. to suppress

ritual
[rich′ oo əl]

n. 1. a set procedure for a religious or other ceremony
2. a custom; a routine
adj. 1. ceremonial
2. customary; routine

viable
[vī′ ə bəl]

adj. 1. practicable; possible
2. capable of living or developing

WORDS TO WATCH

Which words would you like to practice with a bit more? Pick 3–5 words to study and list them below. Write the word, its definition, and compose your own sentence using the word correctly. This extra practice could be the final touch to learning a word.

	Word	Definition	Your Sentence
1.			
2.			
3.			
4.			
5.			

27 Geology

Above and Below

The Australian **hinterland**, known as the Outback, is one of the harshest environments on Earth. The desert receives little rain and summer temperatures can reach 115° F (45° C),
5 with averages around 90° F. The wonder of the region is Uluru, a huge red sandstone **monolith** that rises 1,150 feet (350 meters) above the plain. In 1872, the explorer William Gosse named the monolith Ayers Rock after a South
10 Australian politician who supported his escapades. Uluru is the Aboriginal name for the rock. The rock has been a sacred site for

the Aborigines who have lived in the area for 20,000 years. In 1985 the rock was made part of a national park, and the name of the rock was officially recognized as Uluru. The word Uluru can be
15 roughly translated as "mother of the earth." Except for the rock grouping Kata Tjuta 19 miles away, the land around *Uluru* is flat, which heightens the impressive nature of the rock. The monolith is the result of 600 million years of physical forces. Though the huge rock may look **impervious** to weather conditions, wind, sand, and rain **erosion** still play a part in shaping the rock by wearing holes in its surface. The beauty of the rock needs to be appreciated throughout the day. The changing light makes
20 the rock look brown during the day, but as the sun sets the rock turns red, purple, and orange. Today thousands of visitors climb the rock and enjoy the tourist facilities nearby. Those with **acrophobia**, however, are discouraged from climbing the rock as the **ascent** is made by holding on to a chain link fence. Several people have had to be rescued from the rock. It has not, however, been a fear of heights that has caused more people to refrain from the climb. The rock is considered a sacred site to the
25 Aborigines and they prefer people not to climb it, and each year more visitors are respecting their wishes.

    The Grand Canyon is a marvel of nature. In its layers of rock over two billion years of geology are recorded. The scale of the canyon is impressive. On average the
30 canyon is one mile (1.6 km) deep, nine miles (15 km) wide, and it runs for 280 miles (450 km). Located in northern Arizona, temperatures at the Grand Canyon fluctuate from over 100° F (38° C) in the summer to 0° F (-18° C) in the winter. The eight-mile **descent** on
35 switchback trails takes one through several environments. Every 1,000 vertical feet is equal to 300 miles of southward travel. The region is an **oasis** for diverse animal populations from mountain species like bighorn sheep to desert animals like rattlesnakes. The erosive forces of the

40 Colorado River formed the canyon. Six million years ago the river began wearing away the rocky surface at about one hundredth of an inch (2.5 mm) a year. At one point the canyon was nothing more than a **ravine,** but over millions of years the narrow valley grew. The walls of the canyon reveal the **permutations** the area has gone through. Plankton fossils embedded in the rocks show that the region was once under the sea and other layers expose the area as having been part of a mountain range. Like
45 Uluru, the beauty of the canyon can best be valued with the changing light. The canyon rocks are usually red, but dawn gives them a gold and silver hue and sunset turns them bright red. A portion of the canyon was made a national park in 1919, and the park gets well over a million visitors a year. Many of these visitors would surely agree with the geologist Francois E. Matthes: "Whoever stands upon the brink of the Grand Canyon beholds a spectacle unrivaled on this earth."

▌▌▌▌▌ PREDICTING

For each set, write the definition on the line next to the word to which it belongs. If you are unsure, return to the reading on page 166, and underline any context clues you find. After you've made your predictions, check your answers against the Word List on page 171. Place a checkmark in the box next to each word whose definition you missed. These are the words you'll want to study closely.

SET ONE

| a large single block of stone | incapable of being influenced | a fear of heights |
| back country | the process by which the surface of the earth is worn away | |

❑ 1. **hinterland** (line 1) _____

❑ 2. **monolith** (line 7) _____

❑ 3. **impervious** (line 17) _____

❑ 4. **erosion** (line 18) _____

❑ 5. **acrophobia** (line 21) _____

SET TWO

| a narrow valley | a downward slope | a rising or climbing movement | alterations | a refuge |

❑ 6. **ascent** (line 22) _____

❑ 7. **descent** (line 34) _____

❑ 8. **oasis** (line 37) _____

❑ 9. **ravine** (line 42) _____

❑ 10. **permutations** (line 43) _____

1 Put a T for true or F for false next to each statement.

_____ 1. Using a shield made of paper would make a person impervious.

_____ 2. It is dangerous for children to play near ravines.

_____ 3. One can slide down a hill during an ascent.

_____ 4. If a woman has climbed the 20 highest peaks in North America, she probably has acrophobia.

_____ 5. A teenager's bedroom can be an oasis from the stresses of school and relationships.

_____ 6. You could possibly slide down a hill during a descent.

_____ 7. New York City is considered the hinterland of the United States.

_____ 8. Usually the erosion of a mountain is easy to see on a day to day basis.

_____ 9. An essay can go through many permutations before a student is ready to hand it in.

_____10. A statue sitting on the corner of a person's desk could be called a monolith.

2 Match the quotation to the word it best illustrates. Use each word once.

VOCABULARY LIST

impervious	acrophobia	ravine	ascent	descent
hinterland	oasis	monolith	erosion	permutations

1. "I tried to convince my father to let me go to the concert, but he wouldn't let me."

_____

2. "The statues on Easter Island are so impressive." _____

3. "I'm afraid to look over the side of the building; we are on the 20th floor." _____

4. "This café is my lunch-hour refuge from the stresses of work." _____

5. "The heavy rains this winter wore away a lot of the soil on the hillside."_____

6. "I am going to get away this summer; I am going to the Yukon in Canada." _____

7. "There have been so many alterations to the plan that I am not sure what time to pick up Athena."

_____

8. "Though it was steep, the climb was well worth the view." _____

9. "I'm a bit afraid of going down. There are several loose rocks on the path." _____

10. "We are going to have to leap across this one." _____

3 Circle the word that correctly completes each sentence.

1. The latest (permutation, ascent) in the City Hall redesign plan shows a swimming pool replacing a parking lot.

2. The (ascent, erosion) of the mountain took all day. We set up camp near the top just before dark.

3. I hadn't realized I suffered from (oasis, acrophobia) until we took a hot air balloon ride. I was terrified the whole ride.

4. I am excited about my vacation to the (monolith, hinterland) of the African jungle. It will be great to get away from civilization.

5. Luckily our tent was (permutation, impervious) to water because it rained all night.

6. The (descent, ascent) wasn't that hard since we slid down most of the snow-covered mountain.

7. The nomads were pleased to come across the (ravine, oasis); they were getting thirsty.

8. We had to pull Conrad out of the (ravine, monolith). He wasn't looking and he fell in.

9. The (erosion, descent) caused by the wind has made the rocks into interesting shapes.

10. The new black skyscraper has aptly been called a(n) (acrophobia, monolith). It is so massive it dominates the downtown skyline.

WORD WISE

Collocations

Manifest Destiny was the belief that it was inescapable for the United States to expand westward during the 1800s. (Chapter 26)

At work it can be important to *quell a rumor* before too many people get a wrong idea. (Chapter 26)

Word Pairs

Ascent/Descent: Ascent (Chapter 27) means "a rising or climbing movement." Descent (Chapter 27) means "a downward slope." The ascent was steep and I started breathing hard, but the view from the top was worth it. I hope that the descent will be easier; maybe I can roll down part of the hill.

Where Did It Come From?

Acrophobia (Chapter 27): comes from the Greek *akros* "at the end, the top" plus *phobia* "fear of." Together they join to make "a fear of heights."

Write a letter home about an imaginary trip you are taking at either Uluru or the Grand Canyon. Use at least six of the vocabulary words in your letter.

_____

_____

_____

_____

_____

_____

_____

_____

_____

_____

_____

HINT

Reading for Pleasure: Nonfiction

It might sound obvious, but many people forget that reading for fun makes a better reader overall. If you think you don't like to read, search for reading material about a subject that interests you. Textbooks are not always the most exciting reading material, so don't give up if you don't enjoy what you are currently required to read. If you like to read about true-life events, try some of these ideas to find nonfiction that will interest you.

- To keep up on current events become a newspaper or weekly newsmagazine reader.
- Subscribe to a magazine related to one of your hobbies. There are magazines devoted to almost every hobby including cars, cooking, computers, gardening, and about any sport you can imagine.
- Pick up a biography or autobiography about a person who interests you.
- If there is a time period that interests you, nonfiction books deal with events from ancient Egypt to the unknown future.
- To learn more about a country you are interested in, look for books about the history, people, or environment of the area.

Visit the library to try different types of reading material. It's free! Also explore the Internet for various reading sources. Finding the type of reading material that is right for your personality and interests will make reading fun, will lead to better reading skills, and will even make mandatory reading more productive.

▌▌▌▌ WORD LIST

acrophobia
[ak′ rə fō′ bē ə]
n. a fear of heights

ascent
[ə sent′]
n. 1. a rising or climbing movement
2. movement upward; advancement

descent
[di sent′]
n. 1. a downward slope
2. a decline; a fall; a drop
3. origin

erosion
[i rō′ zhən]
n. the process by which the surface of the earth is worn away by the action of water, winds, waves, etc.

hinterland
[hin′ ter land′]
n. back country; the remote or less developed parts of a country

impervious
[im pûr′ vē əs]
adj. 1. incapable of being injured, impaired, or influenced
2. not permitting passage

monolith
[mon′ ə lith]
n. 1. a large single block of stone
2. a column or large statue formed from a single block of stone
3. something having a uniform, massive, or inflexible character

oasis
[ō ā′ sis]
n. 1. a refuge, as from work or stress
2. a fertile area in a desert region, usually having a spring or well

permutation
[pûr′ myoo tā′ shən]
n. alteration; transformation

ravine
[rə vēn′]
n. a narrow, steep-sided valley, usually eroded by running water

▌▌▌▌ WORDS TO WATCH

Which words would you like to practice with a bit more? Pick 3–4 words to study and list them below. Write the word, its definition, and compose your own sentence using the word correctly. This extra practice could be the final touch to learning a word.

	Word	Definition	Your Sentence
1.			
2.			
3.			
4.			

CHAPTER 28

Business

Shopping Made Easier

One of a merchant's goals is to **garner consumer** confidence. Customers will spend their money if they feel comfortable in a shopping environment. There are several ways stores can be designed to better accommodate consumers' needs.

Businesses need to allow sufficient space between the aisles. Studies have found that if customers accidentally brush up against each other it **detracts** from the shopping experience. If a customer is repeatedly **jostled** while looking at a product, he or she will leave the store without making a purchase. If the retail space is **conducive** to browsing, then the customer will spend more time in the store, which usually translates to buying more. Retailer's can also **attribute** greater sales to something as easy as placing shopping baskets throughout a store, not just at the entrance. Customers will buy more if they have a container for their purchases. A shopper may come into the store planning to buy one or two items and not pick up a basket. But if a few more items attract a customer's interest and a basket is nearby, the person will usually

pick up the basket and fill it. A customer is limited by having two hands. If the retailer provides a basket or cart that limitation ceases to be a problem.

People love to use their senses when shopping. Retailers need to become **proponents** of the five senses. Obviously, a woman wants to touch a shirt before she buys it, but she wants to do the same with the sheets she will sleep on, and that's hard to do if the sheets are wrapped in plastic. Most stores don't provide a sample sheet to touch, and that's when a shopper feels it is her **prerogative** to make a small hole in the plastic so she can run her fingers over the fabric. Unfortunately, several items that people desire to touch, from silverware to paper, are packaged in ways that prevent shoppers from feeling them. A few stores have noted the popularity of offering food samples, especially for new products, but most are not taking advantage of this sensory-shopping method. Just seeing a package of the latest veggie burger in the freezer case is unlikely to excite a man, but if he is given a free taste, he may discover how good it is. More goods will be sold if people can touch, taste, smell, and hear products, as well as see them.

Another area where a retailer's business **acumen** can shine is at the checkout line. The checkout line is the customer's last encounter with a store, and it can destroy a good shopping experience. If customers have to wait too long, they will not return to a store, and they may even give up on what

236

they have already brought to the line. To quell the anger of the bored consumer, retailers need to make the waiting time seem shorter. A simple way to decrease waiting anxiety is to provide reading material. Grocery stores already do this with magazines at the checkout stands, but it is also **feasible** for other types of stores. Retailers can hang posters behind the cashiers announcing special events (book signings, garden talks, food demonstrations) or provide flyers of upcoming sales on a rack where customers can grab one to read while they wait. The checkout line is also a great place for impulse buying. Retailers should put racks of small items within easy reach of those waiting in line. Few people are going to get out of line to investigate a belt, a bookmark, or a mouse pad, but if the item is near enough to touch, a person might decide to purchase it and be less bored while waiting.

Application Exercise

Visit a retail establishment and see which of the shopper-friendly methods mentioned in the reading are being employed and which are being ignored. Spend at least an hour in the store watching consumer behavior. What do people touch? How do they respond to waiting in line? Be ready to report your findings to the class.

PREDICTING

For each set, write the definition on the line next to the word to which it belongs. If you are unsure, return to the reading on page 172, and underline any context clues you find. After you've made your predictions, check your answers against the Word List on page 177. Place a checkmark in the box next to each word whose definition you missed. These are the words you'll want to study closely.

SET ONE

takes away   to get   a customer   bumped or brushed against

tending to promote or assist

❑ 1. **garner** (line 1) _____
❑ 2. **consumer** (line 2) _____
❑ 3. **detracts** (line 10) _____
❑ 4. **jostled** (line 12) _____
❑ 5. **conducive** (line 14) _____

SET TWO

capable of being done   a special right   advocates

shrewdness   to regard as resulting from a specified cause

❑ 6. **attribute** (line 18) _____
❑ 7. **proponents** (line 33) _____
❑ 8. **prerogative** (line 40) _____
❑ 9. **acumen** (line 57) _____
❑ 10. **feasible** (line 70) _____

⦚⦚⦚⦚ SELF-TESTS

1 In each group, circle the word that does not have a connection to the other three words. See Chapter 11 for an example.

1. advocate   attacker   proponent   defender

2. consumer   shopper   producer   customer

3. push   shove   jostle   share

4. impossible   suitable   attainable   feasible

5. detract   divert   distract   promote

6. insight   shrewdness   stupidity   acumen

7. give   acquire   get   garner

8. right   privilege   prerogative   powerlessness

9. quality   attribute   characteristic   whole

10. helpful   worthless   conducive   useful

2 Finish the ad copy using the vocabulary words. Use each word once.

VOCABULARY LIST

feasible	acumen	detract	garner	attribute
prerogative	conducive	proponent	jostle	consumer

1. The smart _____ knows that to impress your guests serve a Gobbler Turkey for Thanksgiving.

2. It's a woman's _____ to change her mind, but you won't once you try Derriere Jeans.

3. A warm cup of Matthew's Cocoa—nothing is more _____ to a relaxing evening.

4. Making learning educational doesn't have to _____ from the fun. We combine education and fun at Kids Creative Software. Visit us today to see how.

5. _____ points with the kids by serving a cold pitcher of Paradise Lemonade today.

6. Family members _____ each other to be the first to read *Natural History Alive:* give your family a subscription today.

7. You didn't think a trip to Europe was _____ this summer. Think again! Quest Travel has tours for as little as $75 a day with all meals included.

8. You can _____ tomorrow's success to today's decisions. Northernmost College—an institution that helps you build a future.

9. Visit Smartalert.com for books on every subject. We've always been a(n) _____ of brighter minds.

10. Combining business _____ with understanding people. Invest with Quistex and watch your money grow.

3 Put yourself in the following situations, and match each situation to the word that applies.

SET ONE

_____ 1. You buy three shirts and two pair of pants.

a. proponent

_____ 2. At the City Council meeting, you argue in favor of preserving an open area as a park instead of building a shopping mall.

b. detract

_____ 3. As guest of honor, you get to decide where to eat.

c. attribute

_____ 4. People at a party tell you that your kindness is one of your qualities they most admire.

d. consumer

_____ 5. You wear a beat up hat with your tuxedo.

e. prerogative

SET TWO

_____ 6. You study whether you can attend a meeting at 6 p.m. and still make it to the movies with a friend at 8 p.m., twenty miles away.

f. garner

_____ 7. You manage to get tickets to the sold-out concert.

g. jostle

_____ 8. You invest $150 in stocks, and by following the market, you end up with $1500 in one year.

h. conducive

_____ 9. You push your way through the crowd to the clearance rack.

i. feasible

_____ 10. You take a warm bath to help you go to sleep.

j. acumen

WORD WISE

Collocations

Classical music can be *conducive to* a relaxing evening. (Chapter 28)

It is considered to be a *woman's prerogative* to change her mind. (Chapter 28)

If a store owner doesn't have much *business acumen,* he or she should hire someone to take charge of financial matters. (Chapter 28)

Word Pairs

Proponent/Opponent: A proponent (Chapter 28) is "one who argues in favor of something." An opponent is "one who is against something." The proponent argued for the benefits of an extended after school program. His opponent said the plan was too expensive.

Where Did It Come From?

Acumen (Chapter 28): comes from Latin *acumen* "a point, sting," which has a root in *acuere* "to sharpen." Acumen then means "keen insight; sharpness."

Put yourself in the consumer's frame of mind. Come up with a product and write a sales pitch for it using at least six of the vocabulary words. Be creative; think about the types of products likely to generate interest among your friends and family.

_____

_____

_____

_____

_____

_____

_____

_____

_____

_____

_____

HINT

Reading for Pleasure: Fiction

Reading for fun can make you a better reader overall. If you like to read about the imaginary, try some of these fiction ideas.

- Find a genre that interests you. Try reading mysteries, romance, or science fiction to see if any of these styles fit your personality and interests.
- Do you like to read in shorter spurts? Try reading short stories or poetry.
- Find a work of fiction related to your hobby. There are books available where the protagonist loves to cook or to race horses or to use computers.
- If there is a time period that interests you, there is likely a work of fiction set in it. Fiction covers events from the time humans lived in caves to the future when they venture into living in outer space.
- To learn more about a country you are interested in look for fiction by that country's greatest authors. Reading a novel or short story by a foreign author can give one real insight into the lives of the people.

Visit the library and explore the Internet for a variety of reading resources. Finding reading material that you enjoy will cause you to read even more and lead to better reading skills for every situation you encounter.

WORD LIST

acumen
[ə kyōo′ mən,
ak′ yə-]

n. a keen insight; sharpness;
shrewdness

attribute
[v. ə trib′ yōot]
[n. a′ trə byōot′]

v. 1. to regard as resulting from a
specified cause
2. to consider as a quality of the
person or thing indicated
n. 1. a quality or characteristic
belonging to a person or
thing
2. an object associated with a
character or quality

conducive
[kən dōo′ siv]

adj. tending to promote or to
assist

consumer
[kən sōo′ mər]

n. a customer; a shopper; one
who purchases or uses goods or
services

detract
[di trakt′]

v. 1. to take away a part
(usually followed by from)
2. to divert; to distract

feasible
[fe′ zə bəl]

adj. capable of being done;
possible; suitable

garner
[gär′ nər]

v. to acquire; to collect; to
get

jostle
[jos′ əl]

v. 1. to bump or brush
against others; to push
or shove
2. to contend with; to
compete

prerogative
[pri rog′ ə tiv]

n. a special right, power, or
privilege

proponent
[prə pō′ nənt]

n. one who argues in favor of
something; an advocate

WORDS TO WATCH

Which words would you like to practice with a bit more? Pick 3–5 words to study and list them below.
Write the word, its definition, and compose your own sentence using the word correctly. This extra
practice could be the final touch to learning a word.

	Word	Definition	Your Sentence
1.			
2.			
3.			
4.			
5.			

CHAPTER 29

Chemistry

From Ancient to Modern Times

Chemistry is a science that has had an influence on society from the ancient Egyptians to the modern day. Among the first chemical experiments were those done by **alchemists.** From 300 B.C. to about A.D. 1700,
5 alchemists conducted various experiments. Two of their major goals were to change inexpensive metals such as lead into gold and to find the **elixir** of life, a drink they believed would lead to eternal life. They were not successful with either **endeavor,** but they did begin the
10 foundation of chemical experiments. They created symbols for various substances and developed methods of **distilling** and purifying various chemical compounds. Their experiments helped in discovering the essential qualities of some chemicals.
15   Today, chemistry is used in areas from law enforcement to health. Chemistry has been valuable in the field of **forensics** in **analyzing** samples of blood and hair from crime scenes, even for crimes that may have happened years ago. For example, in the 1960s an historian suspected foul play in Napoleon's death in 1821 on the island of St. Helena. Arrangements were made to **exhume** his body,
20 and a hair sample was then taken. Because hair doesn't decay, scientists were able to do chemical studies on it checking for **toxic** substances. **Traces** of arsenic were found in Napoleon's hair, which led to the possible conclusion that he was poisoned at the age of fifty-one. More recently prisoners have been freed after years in jail thanks to DNA testing that wasn't available at the time of their conviction. Chemists have also worked with law enforcement in other areas, such as developing
25 lightweight bulletproof vests from plastics and creating chemical sprays like tear gas to bring criminals out of hiding without having to shoot them.
     Chemistry plays a vital role in health fields from diagnosing diseases to creating new medicines. Blood tests, which serve as the basis of most physical exams, were invented by chemists and the blood samples are studied in labs by chemists. Chemists
30 have created medicines that treat everything from motion sickness and ulcers to heart attacks and depression. One area of chemistry that has made surgery much less painful is the creation of pain killers. In the past people often drank alcohol to
35 deaden the pain of surgery, but chemists found ether to be a more effective pain killer. Later chemists developed local anesthetics such as novocaine that can be applied to the area to be operated on, such as the mouth during dental
40 work. Sometimes the discovery of a drug comes from a surprising place. In the early 1900s

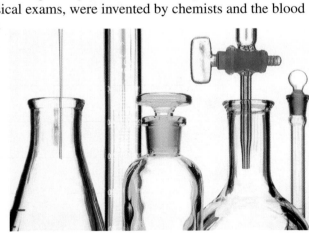

chemists were creating artificial dyes for cloth when Gerhard Domagk from Germany wondered if any of these dyes might work to destroy bacteria. At the time a bacterial infection could be fatal. In 1932 he tried a dye on mice that had serious bacterial infections. The mice were cured. He next tried it on a
45 little girl who had bacterial blood poisoning, and again it worked. Chemists continued Domagk's research to create other bacteria-fighting drugs. Chemistry also keeps us healthy by detecting **carcinogens** in food and food additives. Among the cancer-causing agents that chemists have discovered through experiments with lab animals were cyclamates (artificial sweeteners). After several years of testing, the Food and Drug Administration (FDA) banned cyclamates in 1970. Today chemists
50 are searching for better drugs to combat various cancers and AIDS.

Chemistry has a long history, is present in our everyday lives, and most certainly will provide future benefits. From the justice system to the kitchen table, chemistry continues to play an important role in the world.

▊▊▊▊ PREDICTING

For each set, write the definition on the line next to the word to which it belongs. If you are unsure, return to the reading on page 178, and underline any context clues you find. After you've made your predictions, check your answers against the Word List on page 183. Place a checkmark in the box next to each word whose definition you missed. These are the words you'll want to study closely.

SET ONE

| extracting elements | an attempt | medical knowledge used in law |
| chemists of the Middle Ages | a drink thought to prolong life | |

❑ 1. **alchemists** (line 4) _____

❑ 2. **elixir** (line 7) _____

❑ 3. **endeavor** (line 9) _____

❑ 4. **distilling** (line 12) _____

❑ 5. **forensics** (line 17) _____

SET TWO

| cancer-producing substances | poisonous | examining | small amounts | to dig up |

❑ 6. **analyzing** (line 17) _____

❑ 7. **exhume** (line 19) _____

❑ 8. **toxic** (line 21) _____

❑ 9. **traces** (line 21) _____

❑ 10. **carcinogens** (line 47) _____

1 Match the vocabulary word to the words you could associate with it.

_____ 1. elixir   a. crimes, techniques

_____ 2. distill   b. try, effort

_____ 3. forensics   c. deadly, lethal

_____ 4. toxic   d. dig up, uncover

_____ 5. carcinogen   e. gold, Middle Ages

_____ 6. alchemist   f. small, evidence

_____ 7. endeavor   g. separate, essential

_____ 8. analyze   h. drink, magic

_____ 9. exhume   i. cancer, substance

_____ 10. trace   j. study, examine

2 Finish the sentences. Use each word once.

VOCABULARY LIST

toxic	forensics	endeavor	elixir	distill
analyzed	trace	alchemist	exhume	carcinogens

1. I drink so many sodas that my friends think I see them as the _____ of life.

2. When we toured the _____ lab, we saw some of the equipment used to test blood and hair samples.

3. I was reading a mystery novel and was surprised by what could be combined with cologne to make a(n) _____ substance.

4. The family wanted to _____ Uncle Les when they thought he had been buried with Grandma Allison's hearing aid in his pocket.

5. The _____ worked late into the night trying different chemicals on the bar of lead, but it was still lead in the morning.

6. Scientists are still unsure of all the substances that are _____, but they range from overcooked meat to gasoline.

7. There wasn't a(n) _____ of evidence that Erik had been at the scene of the crime, but the police held him overnight anyway.

8. After doing the experiment, I _____ my lab report to see whether I could tell why I didn't get the expected result.

9. I will _____ to improve my grades by studying more every night.

10. Before the judge could make her decision, she had to _____ all the information the witnesses had given her.

3 Answer each question by writing the vocabulary word on the line next to the example it best fits. Use each word once.

1. If Matthew says he will try to make it to your party, what will he do? _____

2. The police had to dig up the body after they suspected murder as the cause of death. What did they do to the body? _____

3. Gasoline has been labeled a cancer-causing substance. What is it? _____

4. At 75, Milton looked the same as he did at 25. His friends thought he had found the secret to long life. What did they think he had discovered? _____

5. June decided she wanted to learn how to debate. What kind of class did she decide to take? _____

6. The gas that escaped from the factory made six of the workers seriously ill, and they were rushed to the hospital. What quality did the gas have? _____

7. In chemistry lab, Keri had to separate one chemical from another. How did she do this? _____

8. Simon, a young man who lived in the 1400s, experimented with chemicals to try to find a way to live forever. What was his occupation? _____

9. For her law class, Katy was given a court case and asked to study how the jury made its decision. What did she have to do to the case? _____

10. Karl is going to follow his family's journey from Sweden to America in the late 1800s. What is he going to do with his family's history? _____

WORD WISE

Collocations

I will *endeavor to* find out what happened to Fluffy; I am sure she didn't just run away. (Chapter 29)

For centuries people have searched for the *elixir of life* without success. (Chapter 29)

Arsenic is a *toxic substance* that can be found in some water supplies. (Chapter 29)

Where Did It Come From?

Exhume (Chapter 29): comes from the Latin *ex-* "out of" plus *humare* "bury." *Humare* comes from *humus* "earth." The meaning of exhume clearly comes from its roots: "to dig up something buried in the earth (especially a dead body)."

Notice how the vocabulary words are used in the background information and the Forensics Lab Report form below. Use as many of the vocabulary words as you can to complete the report.

Background Information: Mr. Harvey Watson's family has come to suspect murder in his sudden death. They have asked that his body be exhumed and analyzed for toxic substances. The day before Watson's death he spent the morning working in his garden, and in the afternoon he spent several hours in his lab where he practiced alchemy. That night he ate a large dinner and drank heavily. Watson was fifty years old and had no known health problems. The family requests that every endeavor be made to distill the facts as to what could have caused Watson's untimely demise.

Forensics Lab Report

Examiner _____

Date _____

1. Name of the person exhumed: _____

2. Reason for the exhumation: _____

3. Unusual substances found in analyzing the body: _____

_____

4. Amount of substances found: _____

5. Final analysis as to the cause of death: _____

_____

HINT

Play with Words

To make reading and vocabulary fun, learn to enjoy using words in recreational settings.

- Pick up the newspaper and do the crossword puzzle.
- Buy popular board games that are based on using words such as Scrabble, Boggle, or Scattergories. Invite your friends over to play.
- Play word games when traveling—for example, the first person says a type of food and the next person must say a word that begins with the last letter of the previous word: pizza, apple, eggplant, tomato, oatmeal. Pick another category when no one can think of a new word to fit the last letter.
- Write cards, letters, or e-mail messages that play with language—for example, write a thank-you note that uses several synonyms to express how "kind" your friend was: tender, considerate, amiable, compassionate, solicitous, obliging, benevolent, sensitive. Your friends will enjoy getting your letters and e-mails, and they will appreciate learning new words too.

WORD LIST

alchemist
[al′ kə mist]

n. a person who practices alchemy (a type of chemistry popular in the Middle Ages)

analyze
[an′ ə līz′]

v. 1. to examine carefully
2. to separate a material into its basic parts

carcinogen
[kär sin′ ə jən′, -jen′]

n. any cancer-producing substance

distill
[dis til′]

v. 1. to extract the essential elements
2. to concentrate or separate by distillation
3. to fall in drops; to trickle

elixir
[i lik′ sər]

n. 1. an alchemic preparation believed capable of prolonging life indefinitely
2. a sweetened solution used in medicine

endeavor
[en dev′ ər]

n. an attempt
v. to make an effort; to try

exhume
[ig zōōm′, eks hyōōm′]

v. 1. to dig up something buried in the earth (especially a dead body)
2. to revive after a period of forgetting

forensics
[fə ren′ siks]

n. 1. a department of forensic medicine (the use of medical knowledge in civil or criminal law), as in a police laboratory
2. the study of formal debate

toxic
[tok′ sik]

adj. caused by a poison; poisonous

trace
[trās]

n. 1. an extremely small amount of a substance
2. evidence of some former action or event
v. to follow the history of; to discover

WORDS TO WATCH

Which words would you like to practice with a bit more? Pick 3–4 words to study and list them below. Write the word, its definition, and compose your own sentence using the word correctly. This extra practice could be the final touch to learning a word.

Word	Definition	Your Sentence
1.		
2.		
3.		
4.		

Focus on Chapters 21–29

The following activities give you a chance to interact some more with the vocabulary words you've been learning. By looking at art, taking tests, answering questions, doing a crossword puzzle, and working with others, you will see which words you know well and which you still need to work with.

1. _____

2. _____

3. _____

4. _____

5. _____

6. _____

7. _____

8. _____

9. _____

10. _____

11. _____

12. _____

ART

Match each picture on page 184 to one of the following vocabulary words. Use each word once.

VOCABULARY LIST

monolith	oasis	toponym	oust	perennial	alchemist
exhume	eponym	ominous	triumvirate	consumer	ascent

SELF-TESTS

1A Pick the word that best completes each sentence.

1. Emily and Becky finally decided it was a matter of _____ as to whether the movie was good. Their definitions of "good" were not the same.

   a. introverts   b. proponents   c. semantics   d. permutations

2. The kids enjoyed the _____ exhibit at the museum. They enjoyed touching all the animal hides.

   a. tactile   b. intuitive   c. inherent   d. impervious

3. There wasn't a(n) _____ of dirt in the house after Millie got through cleaning; she is a thorough woman.

   a. erosion   b. extrovert   c. acumen   d. trace

4. Once we crossed the _____ the rest of the hike was easy.

   a. neologism   b. ravine   c. triumvirate   d. dementia

5. I would _____ my math class this semester as one of the hardest courses I have ever taken.

   a. classify   b. jostle   c. relish   d. quell

6. Because our government is a(n) _____, it is important that everyone votes.

   a. artifact   b. ascent   c. republic   d. eponym

7. Even though Langston says he is a(n) _____, he enjoys going to parties on the weekends and meeting new people.

   a. monolith   b. ritual   c. erosion   d. introvert

1B Complete the following sentences using the vocabulary words. Use each word once.

a. neologisms	b. dysfunction	c. inconsequential	d. heinous	e. jostled

1. Phil isn't familiar with many _____ related to computers. He was really worried when I told him that I had to buy a new mouse for my computer.

2. I thought it was _____ of Jenna not to invite me to her party, but my mother said it wasn't such a big deal.

3. The jockeys _____ each other as they headed toward the finish line; each one wanted to be in the best position for the final lap.

4. Trudy was scared when the doctor told her that a(n) _____ in her lungs was keeping her from breathing correctly.

5. At first the hole in the wall seemed _____, but when Skippy squeezed under it and ran away, we regretted ignoring it.

2 Finish the story using the vocabulary words. Use each word once.

VOCABULARY LIST

analyze	archaic	attribute	detract	endeavor	feasible	gamut	garner
inherent	milieu	multifaceted	paranoid	qualms	quell	wary	

THE AWARDS BANQUET

We thought our college was going to

(1) _____ several awards at the

Statewide Recognition Ceremony. The

categories we had entered ran the

(2) _____ from the arts to the

sciences. The (3) _____ in the

banquet hall was sophistication combined

with fear. Everyone was trying to look relaxed and confident, but it was easy to tell that everyone was

nervous. I suppose anxiety is (4) _____ in any awards event. People seemed to be trying to

(5) _____ their anxieties through smiles, handshakes, and shouts of "good luck." Everywhere

I turned someone was congratulating me for just being there. I began to grow (6) _____ when

any of my competitors approached me. Were they really happy to meet me or was there another motive

for their friendliness? After awhile, I just wanted to get the night over with.

We were served dinner, and then the awards began. The prize for Best Literary Magazine went to

Newark College. I didn't understand how that could be. The magazines entered in the competition were

supposed to focus on the subject of literacy. Their articles barely dealt with the topic. I decided I wouldn't

let such a ridiculous decision (7) _____ from my enjoyment of the rest of the awards. The next

award was for Best Dramatic Production. Eastern College won for *The Old Plank Road.* The reviews of

that show were horrid. What (8) _____ system were the judges using in making their choices?

The following award was my category: Best Business Plan. Our team had developed a (9) _____

plan that had both saved our local bank thousands of dollars and increased customer satisfaction. I didn't

have any (10) _____ about our winning. When they announced that Montana College had won, I

practically fell off my chair. I tried to (11)_____ what the judges wanted, but I couldn't come up with a clear pattern for their decisions. I had seen Montana's plan; it could have been written by first graders. It didn't seem (12)_____ that we would go home empty-handed, but we did. I didn't know what to (13)_____ our losses to. All the winners had seemed like sure losers. I was feeling a bit (14)_____. Maybe our college had somehow offended the judges. We will (15)_____ to do better next year; we just need a new strategy for winning.

INTERACTIVE EXERCISE

Answer the following questions to further test your understanding of the vocabulary words.

1. Name two conditions that are conducive to a good studying session.

   _____   _____

2. Name a quality that would be essential in a utopian society.

   _____

3. What would you recommend a person do to see if he or she has acrophobia?

   _____

4. If it existed would you drink an elixir to prolong life? Why or why not?

   _____

   _____

5. Do you consider yourself more of an introvert or extrovert? Why?

   _____

   _____

6. Name a belief or idea you are immutable about.

   _____

7. What kind of artifact would you be excited to find?

   _____

8. Do you find studying etymologies interesting? Explain why or why not.

   _____

9. Name a job people should be meticulous in doing.

   _____

10. Name an item that is supposedly impervious to destruction.

    _____

11. Give two examples of things that can be malignant.

    _____   _____

12. What are two items you would want to buy from a bona fide maker instead of on the street?

    _____   _____

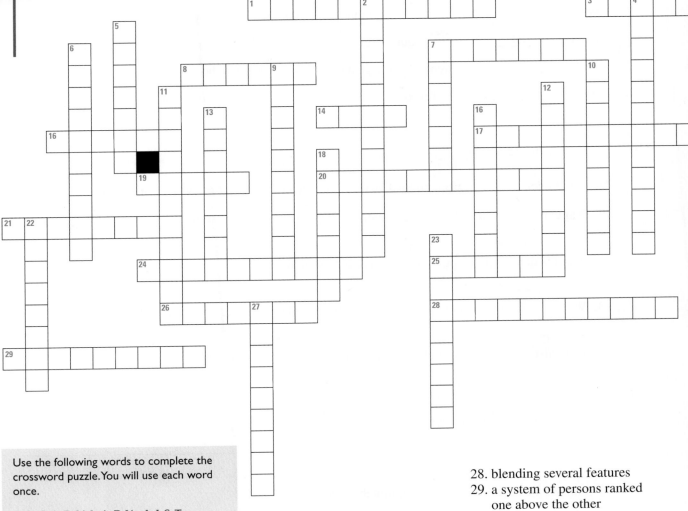

Use the following words to complete the crossword puzzle. You will use each word once.

VOCABULARY LIST

abstract	acumen	bourgeoisie
carcinogen	coin	dementia
descent	distill	ellipsis
epicene	erosion	forensics
hierarchy	hinterland	intuitive
manifest	perennial	permutation
placebo	portmanteau	prerogative
proletariat	proponent	relish
ritual	sequential	totalitarian
toxic	underpinning	viable

Across
1. the lowest or poorest class
3. sharpness
7. to extract the essential elements
8. to take pleasure in
14. to invent
16. capable of living
17. the middle class
19. poisonous
20. transformation
21. madness
24. back country
25. a routine
26. the process by which the surface of the earth is worn away by the action of water, wind, etc.
28. blending several features
29. a system of persons ranked one above the other

Down
2. authoritarian
4. a foundation
5. without any real medicinal value
6. any cancer-producing substance
7. a downward slope
9. in order
10. medical knowledge used in law
11. a special right or power
12. continually recurring
13. evident
15. complex
18. belonging to both sexes
22. an omission
23. an advocate
27. perceptive; sensitive

MIX IT UP

DRAMA

Get together with some classmates to play charades. Use the words below or any of the vocabulary words you want to study. You can write the words on slips of paper and pick them out of a bowl or use your flash cards. One person picks a word and the other people try to guess what word the person is acting out. You cannot use any words or sounds as you act out the word.

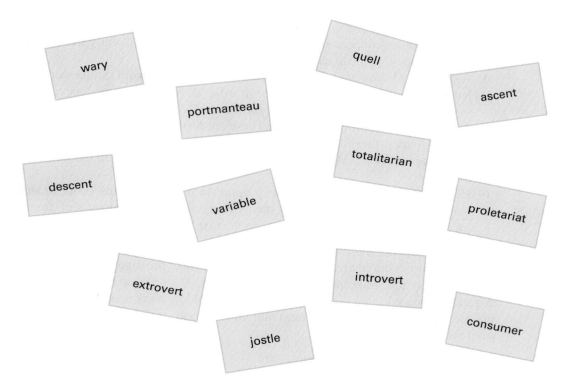

wary

quell

portmanteau

ascent

totalitarian

descent

variable

proletariat

extrovert

introvert

consumer

jostle

CREATE YOUR OWN FLASH CARDS

Using flash cards can be an immensely helpful way to study vocabulary words. The process of making the flash cards will aid you in remembering the meanings of the words. Index cards work well as flash cards or you may use the following pages of flash card templates to get you started. Put the word and the pronunciation on the front of the card. Elements you may want to include on the back of the card will vary according to the word and your preferred learning style. Consider the ideas below and find what works best for you.

1. **The part of speech:** Write an abbreviation for the part of speech, such as *n.* for noun or *v.* for verb. This addition will help when you are writing sentences.
2. **A simple definition:** Use the definitions in the book or modify them to something that has meaning for you. Use a definition you can remember.
3. **A sentence:** Make up your own sentence that correctly uses the word. Try to use a context clue to help you remember the word. It might help to put yourself or friends in the sentences to personalize your use of the word. If you really like a sentence from the book, you can use that too.
4. **A drawing:** If you are a visual learner, try drawing the word. Some words especially lend themselves to this method. Your drawing doesn't have to be fancy; it should just help you remember the meaning of the word.
5. **A mnemonic (ni mon' ik) device:** These are methods to help your memory. They can be rhymes, formulas, or clues. For example: Stationery with an *e* is the kind that goes in an *e*nvelope. Make up any connections you can between the word and its meaning.
6. **Highlight word parts:** Circle one or more word parts (prefixes, roots, or suffixes) that appear in the word and write the meaning(s) next to the word part: for example, in(duc)e. See the Word Parts chapters in the text for more on word parts.
   → *to lead*

Whatever you do, make the cards personally meaningful. Find the techniques that work for you and use them in creating your cards. Then make the time to study the cards. Carry them with you and study them any chance you get. Also, find someone who will be tough in quizzing you with the cards. Have the person hold up a card, and you give the meaning and use the word in a sentence. Don't quit until you are confident that you know what each word means.

Sample card

Front

Back

audible

[ô də bəl]

adj. loud enough to hear

Even though she was whispering, Liz's comments were audible across the room.

WORD LIST

VOWEL SOUNDS		CONSONANT SOUNDS	
Symbol	Examples	Symbol	Examples
a	act, bat	b	back, cab
ā	day, age	ch	cheap, match, picture
âr	air, dare	d	door, head
ä	father, star	f	fan, leaf, phone
e	edge, ten	g	give, dog
ē	speed, money	h	her, behave
ə*	ago, system, easily, compete, focus	j	just, page
		k	king, bake, car
ēr	dear, pier	l	leaf, roll
i	fit, is	m	my, home
ī	sky, bite	n	note, rain
o	not, wasp	ng	sing, bank
ō	nose, over	p	put, stop
ô	law, order	r	red, far
oi	noise, enjoy	s	say, pass
o͞o	true, boot	sh	ship, push
oo	put, look	t	to, let
yo͞o	cute, united	th	thin, with
ou	loud, cow	TH	THat, baTHe
u	fun, up	v	value, live
ûr	learn, urge, butter, word	w	want, away
		y	yes, onion
		z	zoo, maze, rise
		zh	pleasure, vision

*This symbol, the schwa, represents the sound of unaccented vowels. It sounds like "uh."